ADHD Mastery: A 10 Step Guide to Mastering and Understanding Attention Deficit Hyperactivity Disorder in Children and Adults

Implement a 10 Step System to Master the ADD and ADHD Mind, Establish Rules and Prosper for Kids, Teens, Women and Men Alike

Gabrielle Townsend

Silk Publishing

Contents

Introduction

Many people now face serious difficulties due to Attention Deficit Hyperactivity Disorder (ADHD). ADHD affects people of all ages and is characterized by recurring impulsivity, hyperactivity, and inattention patterns. It prevents people from reaching their full potential personally and professionally.

The American Psychiatric Association estimates that between 5 and 10% of children and adolescents have ADHD, with about 2.5% of adults also experiencing its effects. These figures just begin to hint at the wide-ranging effects of ADHD, which impact academic and professional success and negatively impact relationships, self-esteem, and general quality of life.

While the prevalence of ADHD might be concerning, the silver lining lies in the potential to harness one's unique strengths and talents. This book, *"ADHD Mastery: Your 10-Step Guide to Mastering ADHD for Children and Adults,"* is a guiding light for those seeking to conquer the challenges of ADHD and transform them into opportunities for growth and empowerment.

Introduction

This book guides readers in navigating the severe symptoms presented by ADHD, empowering them to effectively manage inattention, impulsivity, and hyperactivity. It offers practical step-by-step strategies and techniques to enhance focus, control impulsivity, and channel hyperactivity, leading to improved productivity and emotional regulation.

In addition, it aims to transform how readers perceive their ADHD. Rather than viewing it as a limitation, this book encourages embracing neurodiversity and recognizing the strengths that come with ADHD. Individuals can thrive in personal relationships and professional pursuits by cultivating self-esteem and building a strong support system.

In this book, we will begin by learning the concept of ADHD in children and adults. We will look into the learning and kinetic difficulties caused by ADHD and provide necessary solutions to battling the disorder.

Chapter 1
Understanding Attention Deficit Hyperactivity Disorder (Adhd)

WHAT IS ADHD?

ADHD is an abbreviation for Attention-deficit/hyperactivity disorder. It is a neurological condition that affects both children and adults. ADHD is distinguished by a persistent pattern of inattention and hyperactivity-impulsivity that impairs daily functioning and growth.

This disorder was first referred to as "hyperactivity," then "attention-deficit disorder" (ADD), and finally, to differentiate between children with ADD but no hyperactivity, either (plain) ADD or ADD with hyperactivity. Medical professionals adopted the new "official" title, attention deficit hyperactivity disorder (ADHD), and its symptoms were published in the American Psychiatric Association's Diagnostic and Statistical Manual of Mental Disorders (DSM-5). The concepts in this guidebook are widely accepted and are used by doctors, scientists, and insurance administrators. The older term, ADD, is still used by the main parent and patient support group, CHADD.

As previously indicated, attention deficit hyperactivity disorder (ADHD) affects approximately 5-10% of children and at least 3-5% of adults. While physicians detected ADHD many years ago, its prevalence was recently recognized. ADHD is often accompanied by developmental difficulties in reading, spelling, mathematics and other behavioral and emotional issues. ADHD affects boys more than girls. Child psychiatrists anticipated that ADHD symptoms would diminish and eventually disappear as children grew older. Still, it is now recognized that ADHD is not a transient childhood problem but rather a serious and frequently lifelong condition with symptoms that often persist into adolescence and adulthood.

THE HISTORY

Many different titles have been used to describe the same set of symptoms that we now refer to as ADHD. The DSM altered the official name of this illness from attention deficit disorder, or ADD, to ADHD in 1987. The hyperactive ADD subtype (named ADD-H) was also described in this older version, and subsequent APA psychiatrists decided hyperactivity was an important aspect of the condition enough to warrant including it in the label ADHD in DSM-IV, even though hyperactivity is not required for the inattentive type ADHD.

This misunderstanding is fairly common, and many popular publications on the Internet frequently use the terms ADHD and ADD interchangeably, with ADD occasionally referring to the primarily inattentive kind of ADHD. Furthermore, some experts believe there may be as many as six subtypes of ADHD. The human brain is a complex organ, and current tendencies in ADHD research are to subdivide complicated sets of symptoms such as ADHD into more precise subgroups. Given the diversity across ADHD subtypes or presentations, it is not surprising that the terminology will be modified in the future.

Naturally, when something has been there for a long period, it develops a variety of names. The symptoms currently known as ADHD were described long before the term was coined. The disorder was first recognized in the nineteenth century, with psychologist William James' description of youngsters with "explosive will" (1890) or German physician and poet Heinrich Hoffman's poem "The Story of Fidgety Philip" (1847), both of which described hyperactive children. In 1902, George Still, an English pediatrician, presented to the Royal Society of Medicine cases from his clinical practice of children who he described as having a "defect of moral control" and "volitional inhibition" that he believed had a biological basis rather than being a purely social or ethical failing (despite using the term moral).

Dr. Still addressed the Royal Society of children who, despite a wonderful upbringing, had behavioral issues from a young age, such as a lack of respect, disobedience of authority, difficulties controlling negative behaviors even when chastised, and major problems with sustaining attention. He also noticed that close relatives shared these traits and had greater issues with alcoholism and the law than the typical person. Dr. Still also observed that this collection of symptoms was more prevalent in male children than in female youngsters. He also speculated that the disease could be tied to early brain damage.

Twenty years later, researchers in the United States found identical symptoms in youngsters who had suffered from encephalitis, an infection-caused brain swelling. The encephalitis pandemic of 1917-1918 resulted in many youngsters with these symptoms, who had survived the infection without visible harm but frequently suffered from concentration and behavioral issues.

3

The discovery of ADHD symptoms in children exposed to encephalitis and in other cases with a known history of brain trauma led Alfred Strauss and his associates to propose the concept of minimal brain damage (MBI) as the etiology of ADHD in the 1940s. As identical symptoms were identified in youngsters with no apparent history of brain trauma, the term minimal brain dysfunction (MBD) developed.

The concept of a biological basis for ADHD-like behaviors emerged far earlier—at least in North America—than a biological basis for other disorders perceived to have a moral component, such as alcoholism and other addictions. Dr. Charles Bradley's finding in 1937 that children with ADHD reacted effectively to treatment with Benzedrine, a stimulant medicine in the form of amphetamine, was another early contribution to the understanding of ADHD as an illness having a predominantly biological foundation. Bradley discovered that Benzedrine, routinely inhaled as a decongestant and anti-asthmatic medication, had a soothing effect on his patients with "organic behavior syndrome." Dr. Bradley noted they could focus more effectively and were less impulsive for a few hours after taking Benzedrine.

Doctors observed ADHD-like symptoms in many people with no history or evidence of brain trauma over the next three decades (1940-1970), and the label of minimal brain dysfunction was replaced by more developmental labels such as "hyperactive child syndrome," "hyperkinesis" (abnormally high motion and muscular movement, sometimes uncontrollable), and, in the second edition of the DSM, "hyperkinetic reaction of childhood." These labels highlighted hyperactivity, impulsivity, and a lack of concentration as symptoms. The move in terminology from attention deficit disorder to attention-deficit/hyperactivity disorder was part of this shift in understanding.

While certain changes in the brains of people with and without ADHD have been found, they are not conclusive enough to determine the presence or absence of ADHD. The illness has a biological basis, but there is no indication of brain injury in most instances. Substantial evidence of heritability—the condition in brothers, sisters, and close relatives—implies that a disorder has a genetic component, even when family environment is considered.

THE RECENT SURGE IN THE NUMBER OF ADHD DIAGNOSES

Current estimates of the prevalence of children with ADHD in the United States range from 3.5% to 7%, with boys outnumbering girls by a factor of three or four. While estimating how many ADHD diagnoses were made 20 years ago is impossible, the number was significantly smaller. Many people have speculated in recent years about an "ADHD epidemic" and whether it represents recognition of a real disorder that was previously under-diagnosed or a byproduct of parents and doctors being overly concerned with their child's normal, highly active behavior.

Many mental conditions mimic elements of ADHD, and some may be misdiagnosed as ADHD, which adds to the misunderstanding over the fluctuating number of documented instances of ADHD. Depression, learning or intellectual difficulties, autism spectrum disorders, and oppositional defiant disorder are some of the more frequent conditions with overlapping symptoms. Finding out that a child with ADHD is depressed or has another disease does not mean that the ADHD diagnosis was erroneous. Attention deficit hyperactivity disorder frequently coexists with the conditions that mimic it.

Various variables could have contributed to the recent increase in the frequency of ADHD diagnoses. The first possibility is that the illness is overdiagnosed, which means that doctors make more diagnoses than there are true ADHD symptoms. Overdiagnosis can occur when the diagnostic criteria for a problem alter, the disease is "popular" and frequently in the public eye, and people present to doctors with a specific disorder that has already been "self-diagnosed."

The second option is that the disorder's prevalence is increasing. This could be due to environmental factors. For example, one theory is that increasing demands on attention, such as smart phones, the Internet, socializing, television, and so on, cause ADHD to be more visible in modern situations than 20 years ago. Because ADHD has a strong hereditary component, the genes causing ADHD may be growing increasingly frequently. This is improbable, though, because allele changes typically take thousands of years to manifest.

The third explanation is that mental health practitioners are becoming more adept in detecting ADHD, implying that the illness was previously underdiagnosed. Many possible causes can result in underdiagnosis, which is frequently the inverse of the causes of overdiagnosis. For example, although overdiagnosis might result from less stringent diagnostic criteria, underdiagnosis can result from considerably tougher and more detailed diagnostic criteria. Similarly, overdiagnosis can occur when a sickness becomes "popular," whereas underdiagnosis can occur when a condition has a social stigma or is relatively obscure or "unpopular." These concerns can be addressed through improved physician and other mental health professional education, more useful diagnostic tests or recommendations, and more effective therapies. Another strategy to reduce underdiagnosis is to offer children and parents access to resources such as psychiatrists, school psychologists, social workers, and educational specialists.

According to a 2018 research of data from more than 45,000 children ages 2-17 collected as part of the National Health Interview Survey, the number of children in the United States who have ever gotten a diagnosis of ADHD is 12.9% for men and 5.6% for females. When the number of people having a current ADHD diagnosis was examined, the estimates declined significantly to 11.5% of men and 5.1% of females, most likely due to some children's symptoms reducing as they age into their late teens or early twenties or possibly due to some initial misdiagnoses. However, a prior study from 2005, using the same interview survey, found that the prevalence of ADHD was roughly 4.2% in males and 1.8% in females.

In the 2018 survey, 14.5% of children with a current ADHD diagnosis were classified as having severe ADHD, 43.7% as having moderate ADHD, and 41.8% as having mild ADHD. Furthermore, 62% of children with a current ADHD diagnosis (equal to around 3.3 million children in the United States) were taking ADHD medication. Less than two-thirds (63.8%) of children with a current ADHD diagnosis reported at least one co-occurring disorder, such as anxiety or depression. According to the survey results, the frequency of ADHD diagnoses in the United States has nearly tripled in less than 15 years, prompting many to assume that ADHD is greatly overdiagnosed. And, given the current number of youngsters receiving medication (over 3 million), many believe that ADHD is also being over-medicated.

Chapter 2
Different Types Of Attention-Deficit/Hyperactivity Disorder (Adhd)

Attention-Deficit/Hyperactivity Disorder (ADHD) is a complex neurodevelopmental disorder affecting many people globally. As our understanding of ADHD has grown, it has become clear that it does not manifest uniformly in all diagnosed people. Instead, ADHD can manifest itself in various ways, leading to the discovery of multiple kinds or subtypes.

These different presentations, each with its collection of symptoms, are critical in accurately identifying and tailoring appropriate interventions for people with ADHD. This investigation delves into the many varieties of ADHD, notably Primarily Hyperactive and Impulsive ADHD, Primarily Inattentive ADHD (previously known as ADD), and Combined Type ADHD, illuminating their distinct characteristics and implications for persons affected by the disorder. Understanding these variances is critical for delivering tailored support and improving overall ADHD management.

PRIMARILY HYPERACTIVE AND IMPULSIVE ADHD

Typically, hyperactive ADHD is diagnosed in childhood, and the symptoms either fade away or evolve into the ADHD mixed type by the time the child reaches adulthood.

People with this subtype can be further divided into two subgroups because predominantly hyperactive ADHD appears more common in early infancy and tends to evolve to combination-type ADHD with time.

People in the first category have hyperactivity but no attention issues. The second group exhibits hyperactivity and focus problems, but the attention issues are not severe enough to warrant a diagnosis of mixed-type ADHD. As children grow older and greater demands are placed on their attention, particularly in school, attention difficulties become more obvious. The symptomology of individuals in the first category does not change substantially, but for those in the second subgroup, the diagnosis can move to mixed-type ADHD as the attention component of their disease becomes more prominent.

PRIMARILY INATTENTIVE ADHD (FORMERLY CALLED ADD)

Primarily inattentive ADHD may include two similar subgroups: one with significant attention difficulties and one with inattention with hyperactivity that is too moderate to be labeled as mixed ADHD. Some studies feel that severe inattentive ADHD without hyperactivity is a different illness with discrete abnormalities in distinct brain areas. Their theory is that a loss in working memory, rather than attention or behavioral inhibition, is the root cause of inattentive "ADHD," as it is in mixed and hyperactive type ADHD.

Working memory is the type of memory responsible for keeping information momentarily, such as memorizing a new phone number long enough to dial it or a short list of phrases long enough to repeat them. Working memory also includes processing, such as attempting to recall bits of a phone number based on familiarity or using another memory approach. In this case, someone given a phone number with the number "1776" may associate this number with its significance in American history and be able to recall it using a mechanism distinct from that necessary to remember a less familiar number such as "4820." The phone number is likely to be forgotten an hour later unless repeated numerous times, but working memory maintains it "in mind" long enough for someone to accomplish another few actions (such as pulling out a cell phone and bringing up the dial screen) before phoning it.

A lack of working memory might impair the selective component of attention, which involves choosing a specific thing to remember and manipulating it in one's mind. This would cause issues with the executive function's working memory. The ability to control and execute plans and intents is called executive function. Making a phone call, for example, could entail deciding to make the call, employing working memory to keep that intention and a phone number in mind, and redirecting attention away from other distractions like television long enough to complete the call. In someone with inattentive ADHD, difficulty remembering things could lead to stronger, more frequent boredom. This ADHD notion differentiates between boredom and distraction. People with inattentive ADHD may struggle to pay attention because they are easily bored, but persons with mixed type ADHD and maybe hyperactive type ADHD are readily distracted by external cues. These people struggle with the third component of executive function, restricting attention to distracting factors.

It is unclear if all kinds of ADHD are manifestations of the same condition or distinct disorders.

COMBINED TYPE ADHD

Type Combination ADHD is one of the three basic subtypes of Attention-Deficit/Hyperactivity Disorder (ADHD). It is also known as ADHD, Combined Presentation. This is the most prevalent kind, and symptoms of inattention and hyperactivity-impulsivity characterize it.

Individuals with Combined Type ADHD face a wide range of difficulties in their daily lives. They may struggle to maintain concentration and are frequently distracted or forgetful. Completing tasks or following directions may be difficult due to their inattentive symptoms.

Simultaneously, they may exhibit hyperactive and impulsive behaviors such as restlessness, fidgeting, and an inability to sit when anticipated. They may interrupt others' conversations and have difficulty waiting their time.

The combination of these symptoms can have serious academic, social, and occupational consequences. Children with Combined Type ADHD may struggle in school owing to poor focus and organization, whereas adults with Combined Type ADHD may find it difficult to maintain employment or relationships due to impulsive conduct.

Chapter 3
The Characteristics Of Attention Deficit Hyperactivity Disorder

In various ways, explaining the features of children with attention deficit hyperactivity disorder (ADHD) is difficult. This is partly due to the fact that many of the symptoms are present in all children and adults at some point. As a result, parents who read this chapter are likely to think that all of their children have ADHD. Before we begin, it is important to note that the features described are not abnormal in and of themselves; they are only bad when excessive.

ADHD children are distinguished by their symptoms' intensity, persistence, and patterning. This chapter will also review other disorders common in children with ADHD, such as learning impairments and severe behavioral problems. This is significant since they necessitate distinct treatment approaches. Impaired reading, writing expression, or math skills are examples of learning disabilities. According to studies, between 25 and 40% of ADHD youngsters have special learning impairments (this will be discussed in depth in chapter five).

Oppositional defiant disorder (ODD) is a psychiatric and behavioral disease in which children are continually angry, disputing, stubborn, defying adults, purposely unpleasant, and even nasty and vindictive. Conduct disorder (CD) is even more problematic, distinguished by early aggression, fighting, truancy, lying, stealing, and property destruction. Numerous studies, commonly conducted in clinics where children are frequently referred by schools and social services, have typically indicated a significantly elevated frequency of both illnesses. Figures vary slightly, but on average, 40 to 50 percent or more of ADHD youngsters have ODD, and more than 15 percent have CD. However, clinics are more likely to see severe instances of ADHD. ODD and CD are less common in ADHD children sent to private practitioners by their parents. These circumstances will be covered in greater detail later in the chapter.

Of course, this chapter should not be used for diagnosis. However, a parent can use it as a "screening" tool to determine whether a child's conduct deserves review by an expert. The specialist can assess whether the child's symptoms are more severe than those of other children his or her age, whether the pattern of symptoms is consistent with ADHD or a comparable disorder, and whether there is a problem. Only a clinician who has tested numerous children can determine whether a youngster has ADHD. Parents who attempt to establish the diagnosis independently are similar to medical students who, after reading about disease symptoms in textbooks, believe they have contracted smallpox, leprosy, and cancer within a few weeks. (Fortunately, the medical students recuperate at the same rate.)

Parents who suspect their restless, clumsy, distractible, and demanding child has ADHD should consult a qualified professional to diagnose and assess whether treatment is required.

Finally, because the list of characteristics described here is not designed to be exhaustive, it will include some qualities present in some but not all children with ADHD. Furthermore, ADHD is three times more common in boys than in girls, and girls often, but not always, have less hyperactivity, fewer behavioral issues, and are less likely to have conduct disorder and aggression.

ATTENTION DIFFICULTIES AND DISTRACTIBILITY

The easiness of distraction or shortness of attention is a characteristic of ADHD children that is virtually always present. This issue is not as obvious as hyperactivity, but it is more practical. The child with ADHD lacks perseverance. Young children have a lower ability to focus and perform long and exhausting tasks than adults. The ADHD child behaves like a younger sibling. He is the polar opposite of the person sitting calmly in the corner, painstakingly solving a puzzle without distractions.

As a toddler and nursery school student, the ADHD youngster races from activity to activity and then appears bored. "You can't get him to pay attention for long....," his instructor says at school. He does not complete his assignment... He does not follow instructions." (How might an inattentive student do so when the teacher says, "Take your geography book, turn to page 43, think about the first three questions, and write the answers in your workbook"?)

While the ADHD youngster may have "only" problems with inattention and distractibility, these symptoms "alone" can cause problems at school and in his relationships with other children. Inattentive children may miss the purpose of another child's story and interrupt. His peers consider him to be "out of it." Or the child may misunderstand gaming instructions and make mistakes. One soccer coach we know requires his ADHD player to take his medication before the start of a game.

His mother notes that "he doesn't listen for long... he doesn't mind... he doesn't remember" at home. The parents must hover

over him to get their children to accomplish what they want. When told to eat with a fork rather than his hands, he does so for a few seconds before returning to his hands. He may start his homework as directed, but he will not finish it unless his parents nag him. The child does not necessarily defy orders but begins doing something else in the middle of an appointed task. Tasks that began are only halfway completed. His chamber is only half-restored, and the yard is only half-mowed. As explained below, the child may appear to remember but be hesitant to cooperate. At times, he seems distracted and forgets the task at hand.

It is crucial to highlight that distractibility does not always have to be present. When a child receives personalized attention, he can often attend well for a short period of time. The teacher may report that he "does well with one-to-one attention."

A psychologist may see that the youngster is attentive throughout testing. During the quick office examination, a pediatrician may see that the youngster was not distracted. They are all accurate, but what matters is not how the child can pay attention while an adult makes every attempt to get him to. Many ADHD young-sters can listen carefully for a short period of time. Assume the examiner, child psychiatrist, physician, or psychologist is unaware of the potential variety of such conduct. In that circum-stances, he or she may wrongly infer that the child is fine and that the parents and instructor are exaggerating.

Distractibility in some ADHD youngsters can be concealed by their ability to focus on a single activity for an unusually lengthy period of time. It's usually an activity that they want for them-selves. It is frequently socially advantageous (for example, read-ing), but it is not always. The youngster may appear to "lock on" and be undetected, or he or she may be exceptionally persistent. The activity can be repeated on a regular basis for an extended period of time. Such contradictory behavior in a seemingly distractible child may perplex a parent who wonders, "How can he be distracted when he plays with his video games for hours on end?" The most unsatisfying response must be: 'We do not know, but this is indeed the situation.'

HYPERACTIVITY

Not all ADHD children are hyperactive (which is why the disorder's name was modified), but rather have problems with inattention. However, most ADHD youngsters are quite busy, and hyperactivity is difficult to detect. Many youngsters with ADHD have been overly active from childhood. Parents frequently say that their child was "different" from the start of his life.

Such newborns are frequently restless, have feeding issues, and suffer from colic (intermittent and inexplicable screaming). They also typically experience sleeping issues of various kinds: some youngsters sleep late and with difficulty, awaken frequently, and wake up early; others sleep deeply and are difficult to rouse.

Many of these infants become energetic as they grow into toddlers. Parents typically tell that the child stood and walked at a young age after an active and restless infancy, and then, like a newborn, King Kong burst the bars of his crib and marched forth to destroy the house. He was always on the go, always getting into things, always touching (and so, by accident, breaking) everything in sight.

When he was left alone for a second, he climbed to the top of the refrigerator or appeared in the middle of the street. Pots and pans were swept from cupboards, spilling their contents, glasses knocked off tables, and lamps overturned in the blink of an eye. The mother usually thought, and rightly so, that taking her gaze away from him for even a second was a recipe for disaster: the instant her back was turned, something broke, or the toddler's life was in jeopardy. And she was correct. ADHD children experience more accidents than non-ADHD children and are far more likely to be seen in emergency departments. He is more likely to be involved in a vehicle accident if he earns his driver's license.

The description of the ADHD youngster changes as he grows older: he is always moving, driven like a motor, fidgeting, drumming his fingers, and shuffling his feet. He never stays long at any activity. He takes all of his toys from the shelf, plays with them briefly, and then discards them. He can't color for very long. He can't be read to without becoming bored. Of course, he can't sit still at the dining table, and he might not even be able to sit quietly in front of the TV. He drives the other passengers insane in the automobile. He pokes the people next to him, fiddles with the window switches, yanks on other people's seat belts, and kicks the front seat passengers. His instructor describes him as fidgety, disruptive, unable to sit quietly, gets up and moves about the classroom, talks out, clowns and jostles, and troubles and annoys his classmates. Sometimes the ADHD child is as talkative as he is hyperactive, chatting as he goes.

It is critical to note that what distinguishes the ADHD youngster is not his level of activity when playing. All children make all grownups appear to be sloths. On the playground, the ADHD child cannot be identified. His top speed is not faster than other children's. What distinguishes the ADHD child is that when asked to switch off his motor, he cannot do so for long. Unlike other youngsters, he cannot control his behavior at home or in the classroom.

However, the ADHD youngster does not have to be constantly moving. He can sit reasonably still at times. For whatever reason, this is more likely to happen when he receives specific attention from an adult. That is important to remember since individuals who evaluate the youngster are sometimes deceived when he remains quiet for ten to fifteen minutes. They frequently realize their mistake when they try to extend that period to an hour or so.

To reiterate, one critical aspect of ADHD is that not all ADHD children are hyperactive. There are ADHD children who exhibit many of the issues discussed in this chapter but are not overly active, and there are also ADHD children who are not overly active.

ADHD children make decisions on the spur of the moment. He dashes into the street, up the tree, and onto the ledge. As a result, he gets his fair share of cuts, bruises, abrasions, and trips to the ER. He is prone to mishaps. He ruins toys and wears out clothes without thinking about it. It sounded like fun to walk down the street in his Sunday best; he wondered what would happen if he twisted the toy's knob.

Poor planning and judgment are other symptoms of impulsivity. It is difficult to predict how much planning and judgment children should have, but ADHD youngsters appear to have less of these traits than appears to be age-appropriate. They are more likely than most children to run off in multiple directions at the same time. They are unorganized and disorderly. Their impulsiveness, along with their distractibility, results in disorganized rooms, sloppy dresses (untucked shirts, unzipped zippers), unfinished projects, and negligent reading and writing.

Another issue that some ADHD youngsters have is bladder and bowel control. Some ADHD youngsters may wet or dirty themselves slightly during the day when they are younger. They appear to ignore their "urgent needs" and overflow somewhat. Bedwetting, which affects roughly 10% of all six-year-old boys, appears to be three times more common in ADHD youngsters. Bedwetting in some ADHD children may be associated with exceptionally deep sleep, but this is not proven. The link between ADHD and bedwetting is vital to recognize since, in the past, "accidents" were frequently interpreted as a sign of deeper psychological issues. This, however, does not appear to be the case. Bedwetting is frequently present as a symptom of ADHD and responds to the general medication provided for it.

Social impulsivity, often known as antisocial conduct, can be a concern in ADHD youngsters. Every youngster steals, every child lies, and the majority of children play with matches at some point. Most youngsters learn to control their impulses as they get older.

Some ADHD kids do not; they can take, lie, or ignite matches whenever they want. (When repeated and severe, this may be a sign of a behavior disorder.) ADHD does not explain why youngsters want to do these activities. Children steal for many different reasons. Stealing may originate from a basic want to have or a desire to have items that would buy affection; it may be an attempt to gain status in a group; it may be a source of thrill or a means of retaliating, garnering attention or punishment.

What matters is that if these motivations emerge in an ADHD youngster, he is less able to regulate himself than other children. Obviously, treating such a youngster would necessitate a two-pronged approach: dealing with the specific motive and reducing impulsivity (or strengthening self-control).

Furthermore, impulsivity, like hyperactivity, may be absent. The ADHD child could simply be inattentive. This is significant because impulsivity, like hyperactivity, is quite obvious, whereas inattention may not be.

ATTENTION-DEMANDING BEHAVIOR

All children require adult engagement, involvement, and attention in order to develop appropriately. They require less as they age, but they still require the awareness and interest of people they love and respect.

The ADHD youngster craves attention, yet this is not what distinguishes him. Because of his insatiability, he is unique and demanding. He, like a younger child, desires to be the center of attention at all times. He can complain, badger, tease, and bother you indefinitely. With age, the manifestations shift.

As a toddler, he may repeat irritating and forbidden activities; as an older child, he may strive to monopolize the dinner-table talk, clown in the classroom, and show off with his buddies, putting himself in danger and causing adults distress. These features of his behavior may be hidden because he does not always exhibit affectionate behavior. Many, but far from all, ADHD youngsters have been ineffective. They were not cuddlers when they were babies. They didn't sleep on laps but wriggled away to do their own thing. They were unconcerned when their mothers dropped them off at babysitters or nursery school.

Nonetheless, the same children might sometimes stand at arm's length and prod their parents with a pole. Parents may find the desire for attention unpleasant, puzzling, and irritating. Because the youngster is so demanding, they believe they have not met his requirements.

They feel inadequate since they don't know how to satisfy him. Finally, they are irritated since the youngster can cling and poke at the same time and indefinitely.

DIFFICULTIES IN COORDINATION

Approximately half of ADHD children have difficulty with coordination, which, when severe, might be interpreted as a sign of another ailment, developmental coordination disorder (DCD). Some ADHD youngsters struggle with "fine-motor control": they have difficulty coloring, cutting with scissors, tying shoelaces, and buttoning. Handwriting is frequently poor, and the ADHD child sees writing as a job. A lack of coordination combined with a failure to prepare can result in an illegibly written page with words overrunning lines, the sides of the page, and each other. Others may have minor balance issues, such as while learning to ride a bicycle. Other ADHD children may have poor hand-eye coordination, making it difficult for them to throw and catch a ball or play baseball or tennis. Such issues do not affect all ADHD children.

Many are athletic and have exceptional coordination. When coordination issues arise, boys typically have more challenges than girls because athletic ability is a key source of acceptance by others for boys.

Even youngsters with poor coordination may be able to participate in activities demanding broad muscle groups, such as running or swimming.

RESISTANT, OPPOSITIONAL, AND DOMINEERING SOCIAL BEHAVIOR

Many hyperactive children exhibit three specific features in their interpersonal behavior: (1) a significant resistance to social expectations, including resistance to "do's" and "don'ts," as well as "shoulds" and "shouldn'ts"; (2) enhanced independence; and (3) domineering behavior with other children.

The difficulty many of these children have in complying with the demands and prohibitions of parents and instructors is probably the single most upsetting element of ADHD children's behavior and the one most commonly responsible for their referral to treatment. Some ADHD children may appear to be difficult to discipline. They appear to be two years old in certain ways. Their parents describe them as "obstinate... stubborn... negativistic... bossy... disobedient... sassy... not caring." All methods of discipline appear to be ineffective: rewards, deprivation of privileges, and physical punishment. "He wants to do things his way... He never appears to listen... He never learns from his mistakes... You can't get through to him... Punishment simply slides off his back... He's almost impervious to whatever we do." ADHD youngsters, on the other hand, exhibit resistance in different ways. Some appear to forget what is told to them, but others appear to actively fight what is asked of them. We'll go into the implications of this when we talk about the disorder's causes.

In terms of independence, the ADHD youngster is frequently overly autonomous yet might be overly dependant in a few cases. Independence may be noticed from a young age. When a toddler is two years old, he is likely to wander ten blocks away from home. He is joyful and excited when he is taken home to his worried and distressed parents. He does not appear to be bothered by the separation. He is not the type of youngster who will be sad on his first day of nursery school or kindergarten or when he is left with his grandparents. The minority of ADHD children that are extremely dependent tend to be immature, babyish, and clingy. They are the children who are most likely to exhibit the indicated continual attention-demanding behavior.

The ADHD child's connections with his siblings and classmates are likely to follow a predictable pattern. He was a tease when he was younger. He becomes adept at irritating and troubling other people. As he gets older, he develops a strong tendency to be bossy. This contrasts with his resistance to being bossed around by adults. When he is playing with other kids, he tries to be the leader. He wishes to have control over which games are played. He wants to make the rules, and if the game isn't played the way he wants, he may quit.

Other children tend to shun him, and the ADHD child is likely to be lonely after a while. This absence of friendship is not comparable to that of a timid, withdrawn child. The ADHD youngster is frequently pushy socially, and while he can effectively start friendships, his manner repels other children. He will inform his parents that he is being talked about, rejected, and possibly bullied. These reports are neither excuses nor wrong. They are accurate appraisals of what his behavior causes other kids to do. He "makes friends easily but can't keep them." As a result, the ADHD youngster frequently interacts with younger children. The ADHD child, on the other hand, is not always physically hostile. He is not sadistic and does not love inflicting pain on others. He does have more than his fair share of arguments, but this is due to his impulsiveness and the fact that his brothers, sisters, and schoolmates are usually not thrilled with being pushed around and told what to do.

EMOTIONAL DIFFICULTIES

Many ADHD children have emotional difficulties. The phrase "emotional" is one of those ambiguous terms that everyone uses in different contexts and whose meaning is unclear. Let us clarify that labeling these problems as emotional does not imply that they are mentally caused—in fact, the majority of them are unlikely to be.

Because ADHD youngsters experience mood swings and cycles, their conduct is unpredictable. They have a difficult time controlling their emotions. According to his parents, "he's cheerful one minute and tough to get along with the next... He has good and bad days, and it's difficult to comprehend why." The final statement is crucial. We all have good and bad days, and our moods are frequently linked to our experiences. It is frequently more difficult to determine why an ADHD youngster was terrible yesterday and excellent today.

Many ADHD children exhibit extraordinary under- and over-reactivity. They can be pain-insensitive at times. They appear unaffected by, and are less likely to respond to, the frequent bumps, falls, and scratches that younger children experience. (This is sometimes masked by increased attention seeking. When their parents are looking, they may try to extract every last drop of sympathy they can.) They are frequently fearless. Fearless-ness, a desire for attention, impulsivity, and a tendency not to "plan ahead" is likely to land them in socially unacceptable situa-tions: when young, at the tops of trees; when older, impressing their adolescent peers with taboo behavior and attracting the attention of the local police. Fortunately, not all ADHD young-sters exhibit such fearlessness.

ADHD children's hyperactivity can often emerge as excessive excitement during enjoyable activities. Most young children will be excited by the circus, but ADHD youngsters are prone to become overly excited in such situations. They may even lose control of themselves in less stimulating situations, such as going to the grocery. Excessive irritability or rage during frustrating activities can also be signs of over-reactivity. Of course, most youngsters (and adults) do not cope well with frustration or disappointment. The ADHD youngster, on the other hand, has a considerably lower tolerance for frustration and a more violent reaction to it. When things don't go his way, he has tantrums, angry outbursts, or sullen periods. When they are weary or hungry, many young children become cranky and babyish. An eight-year-old ADHD youngster may react to weariness or hunger similarly to a typical four-year-old.

Although many parents characterize their ADHD children as "angry," they appear to be referring to irritation and a quick temper rather than violence or hostility—that is, hyper-reactivity to minor comparative situations. "He's got a low boiling point... a frayed fuse." He loses control when he is enraged." Many ADHD children are described as cheerful until such outbursts.

Another characteristic exhibited in some ADHD children that is frequently bothersome to parents is "unsatisfiability." "He seldom gets excited about anything, at least not for long... He can't be bothered to do much, and nothing appears to satisfy him... you can never satisfy him." This trait is occasionally developed by spoiling (in both adults and children), although many ADHD youngsters behave in this manner without ever being spoilt. From infancy, their moms may have recognized that they were dissatisfied.

Finally, one "emotional" characteristic shared by the majority of ADHD youngsters is low self-esteem. They lack self-esteem: "He doesn't think much of himself... He believes he's horrible... He thinks he's unique." The cause and treatment of such low self-esteem are described further below.

IMMATURITY

Immaturity is neither a scientific nor a specific term, yet it frequently describes the conduct of ADHD youngsters. Younger children have a lack of social, athletic, and academic skills, as well as difficulty remembering—and acting on—"do's and don'ts." In younger children, the inability to endure frustration (often resulting in tantrums) and a lack of perseverance are common. Finally, certain ADHD children exhibit another imma-ture trait: rigidity or an inability to endure change (such children, for example, will be angry if their routine is modified or their room's furniture is rearranged).

From a practical sense, it is often beneficial for parents to understand that their ADHD child may behave emotionally rather than academically, like a youngster four or five years younger. Remembering this often makes it simpler for parents to deal with their child: many parents do not know how to act toward a nine-year-old with problems, but they do know how to deal with a typical four or five-year-old. If the parents remember that their ADHD nine-year-old is acting in some ways like a typical five-year-old, it may be simpler for them to understand and treat him.

CHANGING PROBLEMS WITH AGE

One noticeable element of the ADHD child's difficulties is that they change as he grows older. The behavioral issues that emerge in a toddler are significantly different from those that emerge in a teenager. This is due to a number of factors.

First, there appear to be maturational changes; for example, the symptoms themselves tend to reduce with age (just as bed-wetting does). Second, some changes occur as a function of learning: the ADHD youngster is more likely to be hostile after 10 years of rejection by classmates than after only one or two years. Third, recognizing "problems" is dependent on one's understanding of what behavior is considered normal for different age groups: fidgety behavior is expected and tolerated in nursery school children but not in second graders; reading difficulty is expected in all first graders but becomes a problem in fourth grade

What is the typical order of difficulties? The most noticeable issues in the ADHD child's infancy and toddlerhood are in physiologic function: he is likely to be irritable and restless and have sleep disturbances such as difficulty falling asleep and frequent midnight awakenings.

During the toddler stage, his ability to do things grows dramatically, and many of them are difficult. His constant "getting into" things and unwillingness to listen—that is, to respond to parental discipline—are the most troubling characteristics.

As he approaches preschool age, his attention and social adjustment issues take center stage. His short attention span, low frustration tolerance, and temper outbursts make it difficult for him to engage in continuous play and nursery school participation.

Teasing, dominance, and other irritating behaviors with his classmates soon develop. These characteristics endear him neither to his instructor nor to his classmates, and in certain cases, they result in him starting his academic career as a kindergarten dropout.

When he begins first grade, his restlessness draws notice: his teacher reports that he cannot sit quietly and that he gets up and goes around whistling and shuffling. Academic issues, while common, are frequently overlooked. First-grade students are not expected to read right away. Bedwetting may now occur. Although he may have always been a bedwetter, bedwetting is only considered a problem when the child reaches the age when it is expected to disappear (typically around the age of six) or when he stays overnight at camp or with friends. Academic challenges and problems with purposeful misbehavior (antisocial problems) begin to receive the most attention in the third grade when the youngster is nine or ten. Slowness in school was previously linked to immaturity or academic unreadiness. However, by third grade, the diagnosis has been altered to learning difficulties or, following testing, a learning disability. The most serious problem is reading difficulty, but the youngster may also struggle with mathematics and be chastised for untidy writing.

Outside of school, purposeful misbehavior is likely to be a major source of concern. In some cases, it might entail deception, sneaking, defiance of authority, breaking social rules, and failing to demonstrate concern for the rights of others. It also usually includes violent behavior such as bullying and fighting, which can lead to illicit behaviors such as stealing, fire-setting, and vandalism. The duration and severity of these issues are widely variable.

If the problems remain throughout early adolescence, the antisocial problems, if they exist, often become the center of attention. They may worsen, including drug and alcohol issues, and even attract legal attention. If academic problems remain, they may now be assumed.

This is not to say that a youngster with a reading impairment will develop antisocial behavior. Rather, if the child has both reading and social issues, the social issues are the most concerning at this time.

It is important to underline that the age patterns mentioned do not apply to all ADHD youngsters.

Some children have challenges at all developmental stages, while others only at a few. The difficulties vary from child to child at any given stage: some will have academic problems, some will have coordination problems, some will have learning problems, some will have social problems, some will have different combinations of these problems, and unfortunately, few will have all of them.

Finally, many ADHD youngsters outgrow their hyperactivity and a big proportion of the other issues that come with it. Any specific ADHD child may progress through the developmental stages outlined and then cease to exhibit substantial ADHD traits at a later period, such as a preadolescent or adolescent. It is, however, impossible to anticipate who will shed many or most of their ADHD symptoms.

In medical terminology, the mix of difficulties exhibited in ADHD youngsters is referred to as a syndrome. A syndrome is a collection of problems that tend to clump, cluster, or move together. It is common for a given individual to not have all of the difficulties associated with a medical syndrome. Some ADHD youngsters, for example, may struggle with inattention and distractibility in addition to the other symptoms we've described. In contrast, most people will struggle with inattention and distractibility, as well as many of the other symptoms we've discussed. These non-hyperactive youngsters are commonly neglected since their conduct in school, such as daydreaming and looking into space, is less disruptive and is less likely to attract teachers' attention; therefore, they go undetected. This is sad because these children are likely to be underachievers in school and appear to respond to the same treatment that is so beneficial for ADHD children with the extra symptoms detailed in the remainder of this chapter.

It is also worth noting that a child who does not have some of the difficulties outlined at any particular stage of development is extremely unlikely to have them later. The youngster who does not have coordination problems when he is small will not have them when he is older. A child who does not have reading prob-lems at the age of seven or eight will not have them as an adolescent.

This optimistic aspect of his development may provide comfort to parents who are dealing with the hardships that their ADHD child is experiencing. It is not to be dismissed, as clinicians who have treated these children and worked with their families for years have witnessed it. As a result, while ADHD is a lifelong condition, its symptoms often diminish to the point that they are insignificant as a person reaches maturity. Hyperactivity is the most probable symptom to "almost" go away.

OPPOSITIONAL DEFIANT DISORDER AND CONDUCT DISORDER

Oppositional defiant disorder (ODD) and, in particular, conduct disorder (CD) are two of the many conditions that can coexist with ADHD. These are more common in males, children with significant hyperactivity, and children who exhibit early aggressive behavior.

The more severe the child's early ADHD symptoms and antisocial behavior, the more probable the child may develop either or both ODD and CD.

ODD may be diagnosed in an ADHD child who transforms resistant behavior into rebellious behavior. This disorder is defined as a "recurrent pattern of negative, defiant, disobedient, and hostile behavior towards figures of authority."

He will frequently lose his temper, dispute with adults, purposely challenge their requests, do things on purpose to offend others, and be angry, resentful, vexatious, and vengeful. Of course, dealing with this behavior is extremely tough for parents and teachers. In addition, a child with ODD is at a higher risk of getting CD.

CD The essential concern for children is "a repetitive and persistent pattern of behavior in which others' fundamental rights or major societal norms or rules are violated." Such youngsters are violent, threaten and intimidate others, instigate physical conflicts, are physically cruel to people or animals, destroy property (including setting fires), lie, steal, are truant, and gravely break the rules of the family and community. In severe circumstances, the youngster may exhibit callousness and a lack of remorse or guilt. Approximately half of CD children continue to behave similarly to adults, regularly encountering police and spending time in jail. ADHD combined with CD is more severe than ADHD alone, and most clinicians believe it should be treated aggressively from the start.

Other disorders, such as anxiety disorders, major depression, and bipolar disorder, may be present in ADHD youngsters. However, it is unclear whether these diseases are more prevalent in ADHD youngsters.

The main thing is to bring to a clinician's attention the behavior that is causing the youngster problems with people around him.

For ADHD children who continue to have problems with the disorder in adolescence and adulthood, evidence suggests that combining the many ADHD medications available may result in a better prognosis. In the coming chapters, we will go into greater detail about therapy and ADHD in adolescents and adults.

Chapter 4
The Causes Of Attention Deficit Hyperactivity Disorder

Fifty years of scientific research has conclusively proven that ADHD is a neurological illness. This chapter will explain how we came to the conclusion that this complex disorder is, at its core, a hereditary biological impairment of brain development.

The majority of ADHD cases appear to reflect improper brain development that begins before birth, resulting in irregular brain structure, inappropriate message transmission throughout the brain, and defective chemical functioning inside the brain. The fact that stimulant medicines, the most successful treatment for ADHD, appear to have a normalizing impact, addressing the imbalances thought to cause ADHD symptoms, is a significant hint into this abnormal biology.

The child's treatment and upbringing can influence the degree of his difficulties, but it cannot cause them. Certain styles of childrearing may exacerbate the condition, while others may alleviate it. However, no parenting, no matter how harsh, can cause ADHD in a child who is not genetically predisposed to it. Because childrearing techniques might influence the severity of the ADHD child's difficulties, changes in these techniques are usually beneficial. Although such psychological treatments can aid in the management of the ADHD youngster, the root cause of his troubles is biological and inborn.

GENETICS OF ADHD

It's hardly unexpected that ADHD is inherited. Every grandma is aware that children have innate temperamental quirks. Children differ from one another from infancy to preadolescence, according to studies of their development, and some of these differences are related to behavioral difficulties as the kid grows older. For example, the challenges that the ADHD child is likely to experience in infancy (colic, feeding problems, sleeping problems) are most likely caused by inborn temperamental variances.

Furthermore, it is commonly seen that certain temperaments run in families. Some families have high-strung children (such as fox terriers or cocker spaniels), while others have calmer youngsters (such as golden retrievers). Any temperamental trait is not an all-or-nothing trait. It's similar to height. There are various levels of tallness, ranging from very short to exceedingly tall. Most persons who are very short or very tall do not have a sickness, yet being 4' 6" or 7' 2" may be bothersome.

Similarly, most levels of high-strungness are not harmful until they are excessive. All of the characteristics of ADHD children that we have discussed are present in all children. Every youngster has a short attention span, is restless, and is intolerant of not getting what they want at times. These features are prominent in ADHD youngsters. They are, in some ways, extremes of the ordinary, just as very short or very tall people are. Their qualities include both too much and too little of certain standard attributes.

In families where ADHD is present, parents commonly tell us that they experienced similar issues when their ADHD child was the same age. Depending on the circumstances, being aware of this commonality might be beneficial or detrimental. It can be advantageous when parents recall the challenges they encountered and the most effective strategies for coping with them.

This may provide important information for assisting the youngster. When parents downplay the challenges caused by ADHD, the awareness can be harmful. If the parents are afraid to admit, even to themselves, that ADHD caused them (or continues to cause) hardship, they may minimize the problems it is giving the child. If this occurs, the parents may overlook major problems in their child that require notice in order to be addressed.

Scientists have begun to investigate the psychological problems faced among close relatives, notably siblings and parents, as they have researched ADHD children. They discovered two significant influences. First, siblings of ADHD children are more likely to have ADHD difficulties than siblings of non-ADHD children. Second, as previously said, the parents and other near relatives of ADHD children report having such issues as children (and, as we will show later, many likely have them as adults). In terms of numbers, a sibling of a child with ADHD has a 25- 30 percent probability of getting ADHD himself, and each child of a parent with ADHD has a 50 percent chance of having ADHD. In short, ADHD is inherited.

Initially, the psychiatrists who made these findings were unsure whether the condition was genetic or not. Perhaps psychologically disturbed parents raised psychologically disturbed children. This is not genetic but rather a sort of psychological heredity.

Not everything passed down through families is genetic. And whether something runs strongly in a family does not tell us whether it is passed down genetically or through learning. All children of Chinese-speaking parents speak Chinese—this is entirely learned. Red hair is a hereditarily transmitted feature that affects a tiny percentage of the children of redhead parents. The difficulty with ADHD is differentiating nature from nurture—that is, separating difficulties caused by heredity from those caused by how one was raised.

Investigators have approached this topic in novel ways. First, they looked at ADHD in twins. The twin studies revealed that identical twins (those with identical genes) are both more likely to have ADHD if one twin has it, whereas fraternal twins (those born together but sharing genes similar to any other two siblings) are no more likely to both have ADHD than any other brother or sister combination.

In other words, genes are really important. On average, if one identical twin has ADHD, the other twin has an 80% probability of having it as well. In a second study, researchers looked at ADHD in children raised by adoptive and foster parents with little exposure to their original parents.

This has enabled scientists to distinguish the influence of genetic elements inherited from biological parents from social ones encountered in the family in which they were raised. Several studies have found that biological parents and siblings of adopted children with ADHD are more likely to develop ADHD themselves, but adoptive parents are not. To put it another way, adopted children with ADHD are more likely to resemble their biological parents and siblings, even if they were not raised by them. The assumption is that environmental variables do not play a major role in the development of ADHD and that the disorder is passed down genetically. However, while these genetic discoveries indicate that certain types of parents are more likely to have ADHD children, the studies do not imply that such parents will always have them.

Although twin and adoption studies have almost proved that ADHD has a genetic foundation, contemporary researchers have been looking for the precise genes implicated. However, this is a hard and frequently time-consuming operation. It may entail researching the entire genome (the entire set of a person's genes) of a large number of persons with ADHD to determine which ADHD-like genes are more common. It could also involve checking for genes known to be important in the development of ADHD in people to see if those genes are present. Alternatively, it may entail searching for genes considered to be responsible for illnesses commonly connected with ADHD, such as conduct problems, learning disabilities, alcoholism, and autism. All of these attempts have yielded results only through the steady collecting of different information from hundreds of researchers. There is no evidence that there is "a gene" for ADHD at this time.

THE BRAIN IN ADHD

A youngster who has ADHD has inherited brain defects that cause the disorder. Key areas of the brain appear smaller and underdeveloped for the child's age, particularly those areas implicated in ADHD symptoms.

The brain may even be slightly smaller overall (but this does not imply inferior intelligence). However, it is not the size of these portions that is important, but how their cells are linked to other cells throughout the brain.

The smooth flow of information from one location to another determines almost all of our thinking and behavior. The brain is an astonishingly sophisticated network of almost 100 billion nerve cells. The brain is similar to a telephone network in certain ways but with one important distinction.

The links in the telephone network are electrical; electricity moves from one wire to another by physical contact. The connections in the brain, on the other hand, are chemical. One nerve cell releases a tiny amount of molecules (such as the previously stated dopamine), which are detected by the second cell and cause it to "fire." These substances are referred to as neurotransmitters. Because not enough of the first cell's neurotransmitter has been released, the second cell will not fire if there is insufficient of that neurotransmitter. Although the nerve cells themselves are intact, the connection appears to be broken. Different neurotransmitters exist in different parts of the brain. If one neurotransmitter is deficient, the area of the brain that it controls will not function properly. ADHD children are most likely weak in certain neurotransmitters.

The typical brain is quite immature and underdeveloped at birth, but it quickly adds neurons and expands to the point when it has too many cells. It must eliminate unneeded neurons so that by the late teens or early twenties, the brain contains largely those neurons and interconnections discovered to be important for functioning in the environment it has experienced up to that point. The person's behavior quality during those years corresponds to these brain changes.

He has limited attention as a four-year-old, and his neurons and connections are swiftly but chaotically proliferating. His attention had improved (but was not perfect) by the age of eleven, and a significant drop in the number of neurons had begun. He has the focus and concentration of an adult by the age of twenty, as well as most of the brain organization he will likely retain for the rest of his life. Most other sophisticated functions follow the same trend, with the brain growing more proficient as it ages. The child with ADHD, on the other hand, appears to act like a youngster three or four years younger and exhibits developmentally inappropriate levels of inattention, hyperactivity, and impulsivity. His brain is similar to that of a younger child, and he is likely to have underdeveloped crucial parts. Numerous studies undertaken over the last half-decade have shown that the connections between brain cells for tasks such as attention that are compromised in ADHD are aberrant and underdeveloped.

These defects appear to have been present since a very young age, implying that it is a developmental process. These undeveloped areas make it harder for the developing youngster to generate complete and healthy cell connections. Even in individuals with modest ADHD symptoms, these areas may be smaller. The coating of nerve cells is likely to be thinner in adults with more severe symptoms.

If, on the other hand, a child's ADHD symptoms gradually improve over time, these areas are likely to have thickened and his cell connections to have normalized. It is also worth noting that neurochemical studies have revealed that the neurotransmitter that conducts messages at many of these sites is dopamine, which is boosted by the stimulant medicine that is so effective in treating ADHD. Even more intriguing, when a person with ADHD is given stimulants, the activity of faulty cell connections appears to return to normal. In other places, the neurotransmitter is norepinephrine, another chemical impacted by ADHD medication.

These anatomic and chemical distinctions are often regarded as inherited, constituting a component of the individual's genetic make-up. Could they also be the result of an error in the baby's development before birth? That example, might ADHD be caused by changes in the chemical or structure of the brain during pregnancy or birth? Little is known about prenatal impacts; however, there is some evidence that extremely tiny birth size—and thus prematurity—may occasionally result in ADHD symptoms. Other changes in the mother's biological processes during pregnancy may also result in fetal maldevelopment. These are covered in greater detail later in this chapter.

However, genetic origins have been found considerably more frequently. For example, our genes govern the majority of the chemistry in our bodies, including the brain.

Qualities such as hair color, eye color, or certain types of mental impairment, like ADHD, tend to run in families, and these qualities are tied to the synthesis of specific chemicals in the body. The quantity and types of these substances are determined by genes. Certain genes may also regulate the levels of neurotransmitters in the brain, and a few genes may result in decreased availability of certain neurotransmitters.

Some of these neurotransmitters are found in areas of the brain that regulate attention, among other things. An overabundance of these neurotransmitters may result in an improved ability to focus attention and inhibit behavior in order to manage oneself. A shortage of these neurotransmitters, which is most likely the case in ADHD youngsters, would result in under-activity of that area of the brain, resulting in concentration issues and a lack of self-control. These areas of the brain are likely to modulate mood and increase appropriate responses to what is going on around the youngster.

As a result, a decrease in neurotransmitter availability in this area would result in a decreased ability to focus attention; a decreased ability to check one's behavior—to apply brakes; a decreased sensitivity to others' reactions—to do's and don'ts, approval or disapproval; and a decreased ability to moderate mood—that is, an increased tendency toward sudden and dramatic mood changes.

OTHER CAUSES OF ADHD

Although hereditary brain abnormalities are not the most common cause of ADHD, doctors have looked into a number of additional possibilities. Complications during pregnancy, preterm, and difficulty giving birth, particularly due to oxygen deprivation, lead exposure, and a mother's use of cigarettes or alcohol while pregnant, are examples of these. What many of these have in common is that they all show potential harm to the growing brain, often in areas known to be linked with ADHD. Some specialists believe that such brain injuries can imitate ADHD but will not cause the entire ADHD spectrum of symptoms in the absence of most of the disorder's genes. Several situations have been extensively documented as occasionally causing hyperactivity, inattention, impulsivity, and ADHD.

As mentioned in the preceding section, fetal development damage during pregnancy, resulting in a low-birth-weight infant or prematurity, is an unpredictable but evident path to ADHD. A difficult and prolonged delivery, particularly one that results in baby brain damage, is also a risk factor. In summary, anything that harms or hinders the growing brain puts a child at risk of ADHD symptoms. Any injury to the child's frontal lobes, the most mature and "thinking" section of the brain, is especially hazardous.

Toxins are another danger. Developmental neurotoxins are prevalent in our modern environment, ranging from pesticides to chimney emissions, yet relatively few definite correlations have been established. There are, however, a few. Cigarette smoking by the mother during pregnancy is one possible but rare cause of ADHD. It is unknown how this occurs, but cigarette smoke is a well-known hazard to the growing fetus that women should be made aware of. Smoking can cause premature birth, which is also a risk factor for ADHD. Alcohol can be a harmful pollutant since ADHD is more common in children born to women who abuse alcohol or are alcohol dependent while pregnant.

Babies born to moms who use crack cocaine and possibly other drugs while pregnant are at a greater risk of developing ADHD and learning difficulties later in life. Finally, childhood lead exposure from lead paint and lead paint dust, as well as gasoline, is a well-known but reducing threat since strict environmental restrictions have gone a long way toward minimizing exposure from those sources. However, lead paint residues continue to permeate our inner cities, posing a risk to children growing up there.

Whatever the cause of the ADHD child's troubles, they typically lead to typical family problems. Some psychiatrists and psychologists believe that the ADHD child's difficulties are caused by family stress. They occasionally contribute.

They are frequently not, but rather understandable reactions to the child's unpredictable and unpleasant conduct. A tumultuous, unsupportive, disorganized family that exposes the child to abuse and neglect, on the other hand, is well documented to exacerbate his ADHD.

THE EFFECTS OF ADHD BEHAVIOR

It is impossible to establish how much of a child's personality and conduct are attributable to his temperament (nature) and how much is due to his life experiences (nurture). By the age of six or seven, his disposition has influenced his conduct, which has influenced people around him, and their reactions have influenced him. For example, an aggressive child (who is not necessarily ADHD) will have irritated others, who may have become enraged and subsequently disciplined and rejected him. The youngster feels rejected because he has been rejected in the past (experience), but he has also been rejected because he is violent (temperament).

A rejected youngster is also more prone to be frustrated and act angrily. Temperament and experience snowball into a vicious circle. We'll talk about the types of vicious spirals that ADHD kids throw themselves into soon.

The following characteristics are common in ADHD children: (1) inattentiveness and distractibility, (2) impulsivity (the inability to inhibit oneself—to say "no" to oneself and follow through), (3) restlessness, (4) demandingness, (5) academic underachievement, (6) hyper-reactivity, (7) low tolerance for frustration, (8) temper outbursts, (9) bossiness and stubbornness, and (10) instability o These characteristics are biologically determined. They are not the result of the child's upbringing. However, these innate characteristics influence and are influenced by experience. We'll go over how this can happen presently.

PROBLEMS WITH SOCIAL BEHAVIOR

Inattentiveness, distractibility, lack of stick-to-itiveness, and learning impairments (when present) might impede academic achievement despite adequate intellect. Even if the ADHD youngster does not have any unique learning impairments, he will find it more difficult to learn than his smart classmates. A youngster must be able to bear frustration in order to learn. Some subjects are difficult to grasp and cannot be mastered without perseverance.

A child must pay attention in order to learn. Intelligence alone is insufficient. If the child is unable to pay attention to what is being taught, he is effectively absent. A child must be patient in order to learn. Repetition, practice, and drill are all required in elementary education. A child who cannot push himself to do dull, unpleasant schoolwork will struggle with reading, spelling, and math. As a result, the ADHD child is more likely to lag behind and become an underachiever. As the youngster falls behind, he will face increased dissatisfaction and criticism from teachers, parents, and peers. His parents will berate him for failing to complete his schoolwork. He may be assigned to a catch-up class or a class for students with special learning disabilities. He will think of himself as foolish and may be called a "retard" by other kids.

The challenges of the ADHD child evolve as he grows older and advances through the schools. For numerous reasons, his entry into junior high school exacerbates his troubles. First and foremost, junior high school is less organized. The ADHD child must keep track of himself to ensure that he goes where he is meant to go at various times. Second, he has a variety of teachers. Because they know him less well than his elementary school teacher, they are less likely to recognize the potential talents hidden beneath his visible flaws. Third, he starts getting assignments that need strategy and execution.

To be successful, no matter how bright someone is, he must approach his schoolwork methodically. He may be particularly challenged in courses that require reading and outlining. For all of these reasons, if ADHD persists, academic issues usually worsen in junior high. These realistic challenges, along with the special psychological problems that some ADHD children acquire in adolescence, as well as the usual psychological problems that frequently strike non-ADHD adolescents, can make the early adolescent years extremely challenging for the ADHD child.

Failure produces low self-esteem and a lack of excitement. Even if the ADHD child outgrows his distractibility and inattention, he may be so far behind and dissatisfied with school that he merely wants to leave. Although he may now be "normal" medically, and his temperamental issues may have subsided or resolved, he is so damaged by school that he has developed a strong dislike for it and may even drop out.

RELATIONSHIPS WITH OTHER CHILDREN

Some ADHD children are more likely to be disliked by other children because of their bossiness, teasing, and "play it my way or not at all" attitude, and since they may not be very sensitive to the feelings of others, they may repeatedly do the wrong things. (This only applies to ADHD children who are bossy—not all of them.) Even if they are not domineering, other ADHD-related issues may interfere with their peer relationships. If the child is a guy with coordination issues, the social problem may be exacerbated. If he is chosen eighteenth when baseball teams are selected, he may have low self-esteem. If he also throws a temper tantrum when he strikes out, his popularity will suffer. To get favor, he may turn to a variety of tactics that may land him in hot water with both youngsters and adults. He might brag, boast, deceive, clown, or show off. As he gets older, he may want to prove his worth by performing the most dangerous and self-destructive actions, such as stealing or climbing to the highest point. Take note of how temperamental traits (demandingness, hyperactivity) lead to experience (rejection), which can lead to erroneous attempts to mend relationships; the resulting social problems may perpetuate poor self-esteem and make social engagement even more difficult.

The same temperamental issues cause further social challenges in his connections with his brothers and sisters. Every brother and sister have moments when they are envious of one another. The ADHD child's behavior, as well as the reactions it elicits in his parents, exacerbates the envy and resentment between him and the other children in the household. All of the issues that are normally connected with these sources of jealousy are exacerbated and magnified. The ADHD child's siblings who do not have ADHD are generally preferred because they are "good children," whereas he is "bad." They get more credit, he gets more criticism, and he is envious of them.

On the other side, because he demands and requires it, he receives more attention than they do, and they may feel jealous of him. Endless squabbling is frequently the outcome. Another unanticipated consequence can develop if the ADHD child is treated and improves.

The "good" children begin to have issues! There are two possible explanations for this: first, they may have previously had difficulties that no one recognized since the ADHD child's problems were so much bigger; second, the other children may have had no problems but have probably relished being identified as the nice children. When their ADHD brother or sister improves, they lose their enviable position and exhibit behavior that is strikingly comparable to a child's behaviors when a sibling is born. They might become envious, act immaturely, or want more attention. Fortunately, this is not always the case. We only mention it because it is upsetting when it comes unexpectedly and is less upsetting when it is anticipated.

RELATIONSHIPS WITH PARENTS

The problems encountered during the ADHD child's growth place a strain on his relationship with his parents. Because of his temperamental issues, the ADHD youngster is often unsatisfying from infancy. The mother is unable to halt his colic, manage his sleep disruptions, please or make him happy. As he gets older, his hyperactivity, impulsivity, and the other behavioral issues already mentioned cause stress in the household.

Nothing the parents do seems to help much or for long. The difficulty in disciplining an ADHD child is probably the most typical parental complaint. The child is inattentive and forgets quickly. He is told to clean his room, but after half an hour (or one-tenth of an hour), he begins doing something else. He is instructed not to leap down the stairs, stops for a moment, and then does it again impulsively. He is not completely unresponsive to punishment. However, he is far less receptive than non-ADHD children. Parents that are tough and consistent will discover that their ADHD child can be disciplined—at least to some extent. Complete consistency, on the other hand, is nearly unattainable. They may realize that he is almost completely out of control if they are not firm and constant. How he is handled will frequently (but not always) make a significant difference. This is obviously critical in management and will be covered in a later chapter.

The difficulty in regulating the impulsivity of an ADHD youngster has various negative consequences. First and foremost, the youngster disappoints the parents. Second, the child's persistent misconduct is likely to irritate the parents. Third, the parents may believe they are inept and insufficient. These emotions complicate matters further because the parents believe they are not "supposed" to be furious at their children on a regular basis. People are not supposed to have a variety of emotions. One should not despise one's parents, one's child, or one's sister. Such sensations, however, do occur, and when they do, people tend to conceal them.

They act as if they aren't there, ignore them, and refuse to acknowledge them. People are frequently effective in these attempts, and the majority of the time, they are ignorant that these feelings exist. Such feelings, however, do emerge from time to time in everyone. When they do, it is common to feel horrible and guilty.

When ADHD parents become aware of their child's furious feelings, they feel even more inadequate, guilty, and unhappy. These emotions are extremely distressing and are likely to result in childrearing approaches that exacerbate the ADHD child's issues. Parents are already perplexed, frustrated, and perplexed since incentives and punishment appear inadequate in discipline. Because of the child's rage, the parents may become overly severe. They may suspend bicycle or television rights for a week. They might spank the youngster too harshly. The parents' awareness of their severity (to a little child!) produces further guilt, prompting them to try to atone by being more tolerant.

This frequently results in a cycle of alternating severe discipline and excessive permissiveness, which is the polar opposite of the stable environment in which the child performs best. It's possible that the child's conduct is causing his parents to act inconsistently, or — and here's a twist — because ADHD is genetically inherited, the child is likely to have one parent whose ADHD symptoms haven't gone away. If those symptoms have been present, he has a father who has been inconsistent, volatile, possibly harsh, and unpredictable. This is in stark contrast to the type of parent he requires: one who is consistent, even-tempered, tolerant, and dependable.

The ADHD child is prone to feel unfairly treated and may harbor resentment. But he only has a few options for retaliation. He may comply grudgingly, following the letter of the law but not its spirit. He might just appear to cooperate. At the danger of more punishment, he may dig in his heels and become negative, impatient, or stubborn. He may try to retaliate by doing something obnoxious, naughty, or hurtful on another occasion. Nobody enjoys being told what they should and should not do. Even if the parent is a saint, the ADHD youngster (who struggles with inhibition) will feel as though he is getting more than his fair share of do's and don'ts and will be more tempted to stiffen his back in protest.

This friction causes issues in other places. As the parent-child conflicts escalate, the ADHD child will get increasingly upset with his parents, yet, expressing anger at a loved one risks driving the loved one away. As a result, his rage may not be communicated directly in some circumstances.

Instead, it may overflow and be directed at a comparatively innocuous onlooker, such as a playmate or instructor. Alternatively, this rage can be entirely suppressed, only to "explode" in mishaps in which they injure themselves or in behavior that ends in shame or punishment.

To add to the problems, the child's behavior frequently causes disagreement and conflict between the parents. Both parents believe their child is misbehaving, and one blames the other for not disciplining or treating the child properly. The father, in particular, is likely to notice that he is more effective at controlling the youngster. He is, of course, less frequent about the house, and when he does emerge, he is likely to lower the boom, causing the youngster to heave, at least briefly. "I can control him— why can't you?" says the father to his wife. "You can't treat him like that all day long," his wife, who spends far more time with the child, responds, and the conflict begins. Many parents disagree about how much strictness and severity are required in discipline. A parent who had harsh treatment as a child is likely to prefer this technique, whereas one who experienced kinder discipline is likely to oppose it.

As a result, family triangles can emerge from time to time. One parent will play the part of the child's defender, while the other will play the position of the prosecutor. The prosecutor parent, who is the odd man out, then faces a new challenge.

He (or she) not only has a troublesome child, but his (or her) spouse is also siding with the child against him. The pushed-out parent subsequently feels envious of his own child. Again, envy is one of those emotions that parents aren't "supposed" to feel but do. A brief meditation on one's own or friends' families should instantly bring to memory numerous examples of the complexities, hatred, and guilt that might result.

Contrary to popular opinion, family troubles are frequently the result rather than the cause of a child's problems. These parent-child connection patterns are certainly not observed in all homes with ADHD children or even in the majority of them. They have been provided to demonstrate how a child's temperament can cause changes in those around him, which in turn can cause psychological changes in the youngster. It is vital to note that the temperament of the parent is quite important in this equation. If the parent is irritable or impulsive due to temperament or experience, he or she is more likely to become engaged in and exacerbate the child's difficulties. Parents of ADHD children must pay close attention to detail, avoid overreacting, and avoid allowing feelings of irritation, disappointment, or anger to influence the child. They must also be especially well organized.

THE CHILD'S FEELINGS ABOUT HIMSELF

Although the ADHD youngster may experience rage as a result of his parents' reactions to his behavior, he frequently experiences other reactionary sentiments that are more self-destructive. Because the ADHD youngster is rejected, chastised, and told he is annoying, he will feel sad, unlovable, and worthless, and he will have low self-esteem. "You are bright enough to do better," his teachers are sure to say. Why don't you give it your all? ... If you cared, you could perform better" (adding "like your sibling or sister" if they went to the same school). He is disliked by his peers. They chose him for games less frequently or not at all. He is not permitted to attend parties or sleepovers. He is constantly teased since he is unpopular and overly sensitive to mocking. His parents are frequently irritated.

They are constantly annoyed, angry, or disappointed with him. Even if his parents do not publicly compare him to his brothers and sisters, he may tell that his parents prefer his siblings. Parental self-control can reduce but not eliminate these feelings. Even though he has thick skin and no one says anything about him, the boy cannot help but see how people react to him.

The reactions of others to us shape our self-esteem. We learn that we are attractive, nice, or brilliant based on whether others think we are attractive, nice, and intellectual. The ADHD child has low self-esteem. This is not irrational; it is rational. He is failing at school, with his classmates, and with his parents. He fails in every key aspect of a child's life. He believes he is stupid, sluggish, disobedient, and unlikable since that is how the rest of the world sees him ("bad and dumb").

Obviously, everything that will assist the child in changing his conduct will help him avoid the repercussions of that behavior. Although a youngster may eventually overcome physiological and temperamental issues, the psychological challenges he has experienced as a result of temperamental issues may endure. He will have observed and remembered patterns of psychological maladjustment. On the other hand, if he can keep the physiological difficulties and symptoms under control until he outgrows them, he will escape many negative experiences and grow up more readily. He will perform better in school and have more positive interactions with his family and friends. His attention deficit hyperactivity condition will not have serious consequences for him. As we will see in later chapters, many ADHD youngsters can now be assisted in achieving this crucial goal.

Chapter 5
Challenges In Academic Learning Among Children Affected By Adhd

For a variety of reasons, a child with ADHD may underachieve in school. Learning challenges can develop in both children with and without behavioral issues. Even when behavioral issues are present, the learning difficulties may be due to an impairment in information processing rather than a behavioral issue.

The most common causes of scholastic challenges in children with ADHD are specific abnormalities in information processing in the brain. These deficiencies, as well as the behavioral and emotional challenges that may lead to poor school performance in children with the disease, will be discussed in this chapter. The link between ADHD and dyslexia, as well as the unique issues of bright children with ADHD, are examined at the end of the chapter.

AREAS OF DIFFICULTY

ADHD can have an impact on any aspect of school performance, although language-based topics are the most typically affected. Essay (story) writing is often bad among ADHD children. These children may have good ideas that they can convey vocally (oral expression), but they struggle to write them down (written expression) in a consistent manner. Their efforts are typically comprised of modest amounts of poorly expressed written material. Spelling and reading comprehension are frequently deficient.

Some ADHD children also struggle with oral expression and are unable to deliver a logical, sequential description of their events or ideas when speaking. They struggle to locate the right word when speaking ('word-retrieval deficit') and may say the wrong word as a result.

Poor reading skills in a youngster with a language-based learning challenge may affect the child's understanding of mathematics word problems. Nonetheless, for some children with ADHD, difficulty with mathematics is unrelated to difficulty with language-based learning. These children have arithmetic difficulty as a result of deficiencies such as poor working memory and impulsivity, which are discussed further below.

Academic difficulty is not limited to a single subject for many children with ADHD but extends throughout multiple study areas. Poor grades in such youngsters may be caused by poor organizational abilities, a lack of enthusiasm, poor classroom behavior, or an inability to connect with teachers or peers.

Poor performance under examination settings is a serious issue in certain ADHD children.

WHEN THE PROBLEMS BECOME APPARENT

Children who have severe processing or behavioral issues may struggle in school from the start. Many children with the illness, however, may manage the less difficult elementary school years and only have problems in high school. It is normal for youngsters with mild ADHD, especially the inattentive variety, to struggle in high school.

Children with ADHD who also have behavioral issues may have more challenges in high school since their behavior increases around puberty due to hormonal changes. ADHD, puberty, and the growing demands of high school frequently cause problems to develop or emerge for the first time in high school.

POOR CONCENTRATION

Because they are often distracted, some children with ADHD absorb and retain relatively little knowledge in the classroom. They look out the window into space, and their minds are distant from the topic of the lesson. Such a child may misinterpret the teacher's directions and become disoriented in the classroom. He might have to call another child every afternoon to find out what homework has been assigned to him.

He may be unaware of assignments assigned by the teacher or deadlines he must meet. His homework diary could be blank or filled with doodling and other scribbles unrelated to the teachings. He may cause disruption in the classroom by talking. He will be slow to begin work, and because he is often distracted, he will frequently fail to complete the job within the time allotted. He may be required to stay in during breaks on a regular basis to accomplish tasks.

Such a child will have a difficult time revising his work at home. He may spend lengthy periods of time in his room, ostensibly 'studying' but accomplishing little. He may find it difficult to stay in his room to study and may frequently come out, citing the need for a snack, a walk, or some other distraction.

Such a child frequently struggles to sustain the concentration required to read a book. School books are not read, or if they are, the child's mind wanders so often that only a small portion of the content is recalled. Reading comprehension is a specific difficulty for children with ADHD due to poor concentration.

While reading is challenging for such a child, no endeavor is more hard on the child's attentional systems than writing. Writing offers no immediate gratification: letters must be generated one after the other on the page with no immediate reward. It is a time-consuming procedure, and youngsters who are easily distracted sometimes regard writing as a form of mental agony and will go to considerable lengths to avoid it.

Some ADHD children can concentrate pretty well in school but lack attention to detail. As the child progresses through school, his or her work grows more difficult, and nuanced distinctions and inferences become more crucial.

IMPULSIVITY

Many children with ADHD have impulsive behavior that might impede learning. Inability to ponder and plan ahead results in carelessness, which can be a big disadvantage while handling mathematical issues. Failure to stop and consider may also jeopardize the child's work in other disciplines. Impulsive children will respond to a question without giving it significant thought. Impulsivity hinders logical and linear thinking as well as organizational skills. (Another impairment that has a negative impact on these areas is poor working memory, which is discussed further below.) Children who are impulsive may also be 'slapdash' in their work; they frequently take a 'near enough is good enough' approach to their homework and school tasks.

WORKING MEMORY IMPAIRMENT

Children with ADHD have impaired working memory, which is a major source of learning impairment. Working memory is a transient (short-term) information storage facility. A youngster can interpret the present in light of his previous knowledge by using his working memory; he can also remember the steps of a plan while he implements it.

Working memory problems make it difficult to interpret texts, follow multipart directions, organize written work, and solve mathematical problems that involve logical thinking. A child with a poor working memory will have difficulty understanding the material he is reading since his mind cannot hold the part of the story he has previously read as he continues reading. The story's fragments do not link, and as soon as he finishes a page, it is forgotten. As a result, he will claim that the plot is illogical or 'boring.' He will dislike reading and avoid it.

When given a set of instructions, a child with low working memory will be unable to remember them. He will forget the task's final steps. Sequencing difficulties may be related to poor working memory or impulsivity, as discussed earlier in this chapter.

The most difficult area for youngsters with impaired working memory is expressing oneself verbally (oral expression) or in writing (written expression). Their narratives and speeches are disjointed and incoherent. They frequently become engrossed in unnecessary details and fail to see the forest for the trees.

In children with ADHD, poor working memory is also linked to reading (decoding) and spelling (encoding) issues. Working memory is extremely important in the early stages of learning to read and spell. This is when the brain creates a "lexicon" of recalled words that must be retrieved while reading and spelling.

DEFIANCE

Children with ADHD who are disruptive in class will perform poorly academically. When the hormonal changes of puberty combine with the defiance associated with ADHD, this becomes a more serious problem in the latter years of primary school or the early years of senior school.

A rebellious child will react negatively to authority figures such as parents and teachers. Such a child will rebel against teachers who are pushy, teach subjects in which the child excels, or teach in a style that is inappropriate for the child (for example, a teacher who expects students to take notes from dictation will not suit a child with poor auditory attention). Adolescent boys with ADHD are frequently resistant to receiving instruction from a female teacher.

A youngster with ADHD typically develops a strong aversion to a specific teacher and then does little or no work for that teacher. In contrast, he might do well for a teacher he admires. While it is true that most children without ADHD work better for teachers they like than for teachers they dislike, it is the child with ADHD's absolute lack of effort for a disliked teacher and refusal to adjust this attitude that is so distinguishing.

Unfortunately, when a child misbehaves at school, attempts to reprimand him may jeopardize his academic success. This happens, for example, when he skips coursework because he is sent out of class or is suspended from school.

LOW SELF-ESTEEM

Low self-esteem is frequent in children with ADHD and can impair scholastic success. When a child's confidence in his abilities is shaken, he finds it difficult to focus on his academics.

If someone is pessimistic about his chances of achievement, he will not make an effort to study. He will strive to avoid humiliating failures by employing techniques such as playing the 'class clown' (to conceal his academic difficulties), disturbing the class, refusing to attend school, truanting, and forgetting to turn in his work.

Repeating a class frequently impedes the educational progress of children with ADHD due to the negative impact on self-esteem. Low self-esteem also causes a youngster with ADHD to react negatively if he believes he has been humiliated in front of his peers by a teacher.

SOCIAL DIFFICULTIES

Some teachers, particularly in the early grades, place a high value on group projects. Unfortunately, many ADHD youngsters perform badly in groups. They lack the 'give-and-take' that is required for group cooperation. They are often self-centered and domineering toward their colleagues. These attributes, combined with their inflexibility and low frustration tolerance, frequently lead to disagreements in group work. If such work is a significant part of the school curriculum, a child with ADHD may have difficulties that impede his academic progress.

POOR INCENTIVAL MOTIVATION

Progress in high school necessitates many hours of arduous study for a payoff that may not be realized for several years. To thrive in high school, a student must be willing to forego immediate enjoyment in exchange for eventual intangible rewards, such as grades on his report card.

This kind of future planning and reward delay necessitates incentive motivation, which is a difficult area for a youngster with

ADHD. Children with the syndrome typically respond to their challenges by criticizing the work ('it's boring!') or by lowering their expectations, resulting in academic underachievement.

These children have a tendency to put off tasks until the last minute. Only when they are under a lot of pressure will they be able to work. This makes distinguishing the problem from a lack of willpower difficult, but a thorough assessment will reveal the nature of the child's troubles.

AUDITORY PROCESSING IMPAIRMENT

Auditory processing impairments are typical in ADHD young-sters. These deficiencies limit these children's capacity to make sense of what they hear. Their brains may be unable to distinguish similar sounds, recall words in the order they are delivered, or comprehend the meaning of language.

A child with auditory processing disorder will misunderstand instructions and become confused when a teacher talks a lot.

Because of his difficulties understanding spoken words, such a teacher may frequently ask whether the child has a hearing issue; however, hearing tests will be normal if the problem is ADHD. Auditory discrimination and processing tests administered by a psychologist or speech therapist will reveal the exact nature of the child's issues.

SPELLING DIFFICULTIES

Children with ADHD frequently struggle with spelling. There are three sorts of spelling errors noticed in these children's work:

- *Visual errors.* These errors sound correct but look wrong. Examples are 'lite' for 'light' and 'grate' for 'great.'
- *Sequential errors.* These cause mistakes such as 'brigde' for 'bridge.'
- *Phonetic errors.* These errors will have some visual resemblance to the correct spelling but sound different when read; for example, the child may write 'lap' for 'lip' or 'goase' for 'goose.'

HANDWRITING DIFFICULTIES

Children with ADHD frequently have poor coordination and clumsiness when manipulating items (bad fine-motor skills). Handwriting in children with the condition is frequently slow and sloppy. Assume a youngster can do any of the movements involved in letter formation in isolation but cannot do so in a continuous sequence when writing. In that situation, the problem is referred described as 'motor dyspraxia.' A child with motor dyspraxia writes slowly and sloppily.

ORGANIZATIONAL DIFFICULTIES

Most youngsters with ADHD have poor organizational abilities. This will affect their academic performance, especially in high school, when professors anticipate and demand a high level of self-sufficiency from their students. Even brilliant children with ADHD will receive low grades if they forget to bring work and books home, fail to plan ahead for projects and study, and neglect to turn in work for marking.

DYSLEXIA AND ADHD

Dyslexia is a specific learning impairment that interferes with a child's ability to learn to read. It is caused by a brain function anomaly that is frequently inherited. Although dyslexia can be an isolated problem in a child, it is considerably more common in ADHD children than in non-ADHD children.

When a well-behaved dyslexic youngster has the inattentive type of ADHD, his learning challenges may be misattributed to dyslexia alone. This is because many parents, and even some professionals, view ADHD solely as a behavioral issue. They make the error of assuming that a child's good behavior disqualifies him or her from having ADHD.

Assume a child with dyslexia, and ADHD is only given remedial instruction. In that circumstance, he will usually make little or no improvement because working memory and attention to detail deficiencies will continue to obstruct learning. The child's self-esteem deteriorates with time, making it even less probable that he will overcome his issues. In such a youngster, meaningful progress is often accomplished and maintained only when ADHD medication is paired with a remedial program.

Such children typically require only a tiny amount of medication to get through the school day. A significant increase in the child's self-esteem and scholastic development is frequently observed within a few days of beginning treatment.

THE GIFTED CHILD WITH ADHD

Because ADHD is unrelated to IQ, the proportion of gifted persons among those with ADHD and those without is the same. The existence of ADHD, on the other hand, poses three unique challenges to a brilliant child.

For starters, brilliant children's performance is susceptible to even low degrees of ADHD. Small deficiencies in working memory and organizational abilities appear to have a disproportionately severe influence on the performance of a brilliant child. Such youngsters may not perform below average in their areas of difficulty; rather, they may perform much worse than in other areas. As a result, even if testing suggests extremely low degrees of impairment, ADHD treatment should be considered for any talented youngster encountering scholastic difficulties.

Second, in a gifted youngster with ADHD, both giftedness and ADHD may be overlooked. This occurs when the ADHD-related learning disability reduces the child's academic performance from above average (where it should be) to average. Parents and teachers may be content that their child appears to be doing at or above average without comprehending the child's true potential. Only a keen parent or teacher will notice if the youngster is underperforming. A thorough evaluation will reveal the genuine nature of the child's abilities as well as his impairment.

Third, in certain brilliant children with ADHD who are underachieving, the child's outstanding abilities may be recognized, but the presence of co-existing ADHD may be overlooked. This happens when a child's underachievement is incorrectly attributed to boredom, "emotional over-excitement," or a lack of motivation. Such answers should never be accepted without a thorough examination to rule out other possible causes of the child's poor performance.

Chapter 6
The Growth And Progression Of Children Diagnosed With Attention Deficit Hyperactivity Disorder (Adhd)

We addressed the challenges that a child with ADHD faces and how these vary as he grows in chapter three on the characteristics of the ADHD child. We also stated that the sequence of problems is not predetermined. ADHD children may outgrow their issues as they get older.

One apparent and logical question that parents frequently ask is what will happen to their ADHD child. We had no idea twenty-five years ago. This question is now less difficult to answer. We are gaining a picture of the changes in the condition over time as a result of fresh clinical information. The data comes from two sources. The majority of these new studies look at different aspects of ADHD youngsters over short periods of time. These studies have been numerous and have taught us a great deal. A growing number of longitudinal scientific studies, some of which began as long as forty-five years ago, have systematically followed and compared groups of ADHD children to groups of non-ADHD children and have evaluated them through adolescence, young adulthood, and, in one case, into their forties.

SHORT-TERM STUDIES

Physicians who have treated "hyperactive" youngsters for many years have regularly observed that the issues in some of the children improve, become less severe, and diminish with age. Because of this type of improvement, several doctors labeled ADHD as a developmental lag. (The inference is that the immature ADHD child is like a child who is particularly short for his age. Both are likely to catch up, mature, or grow taller, although at a later age than most youngsters.) Many ADHD children's more severe symptoms gradually reduce and eventually disappear around the time of puberty; in other children, such improvements may come earlier, while in others, they may occur later.

Recent research indicates, however, that up to half to two-thirds of ADHD youngsters will not outgrow their symptoms in adolescence and will continue to struggle in school, with their families, and with their classmates. Some symptoms vary and go in all ADHD youngsters.

The ADHD child may wet his bed for a longer period of time than the non-ADHD child, but he does not wet his bed indefinitely. Restlessness and fidgetiness may also fade with age. However, and this is critical, even if these symptoms disappear, other ADHD symptoms may continue. Concentration problems, lack of persistence, and impulsivity may persist. Although obvious hyperactivity may have subsided, many of the other issues may persist for years. Many adults continue to struggle with ADHD-related issues. The practical implication is that if therapy is effective, it may need to be continued for many years, if not indefinitely after the most evident and severe symptoms have subsided.

When considering the practical implications of the ADHD child's later development, one must ask: "Is the persistence of symptoms due to the persistence of temperamental (biological) problems, or is it due to maladjusted patterns of behavior that were learned because of the (no longer existing) temperamental problem?" The question cannot be addressed in broad strokes, but a perceptive physician may frequently provide an approximation for a single individual. Because of the persistent temperamental difficulties, the problems appear to continue in certain people. In others, the persistence of symptoms may be due to taught behavior that has now become a habit. (Similarly, a child who injured his right arm and learned to write with his left hand may retain the capacity to write with his left hand indefinitely, even after the fracture heals.) Some persistent symptoms were initially thought to be psychological, but they now appear to be of physiological origin. When adults in their thirties and forties with ADHD symptoms are given drug treatment for the first time, and it is effective, they usually demonstrate greatly improved attention span, increased organizational abilities, and significant improvement in several other areas (accompanied by an increase in self-esteem) that will be discussed in a later chapter.

Medication alters brain chemistry but does not improve learning. This observation shows that persistent organizational issues are the product of faulty brain biology rather than insufficient organizational skill learning.

Temperamental difficulties frequently respond effectively to medical treatment (this will be covered in chapter seventeen). Some behaviors are easier to learn and embed when young and difficult to change when older.

If an immigrant learns a second language at the age of ten or twelve, he can always speak it with the accent of his first language. Children who are exposed to a foreign language before the age of five or six acquire and remember it more easily than clever adults, and they can usually speak it without an accent.

Habits and attitudes, like skills, are learned more quickly and better while children are young, and habits are learned when children are more difficult to unlearn. On the other hand, because some personality traits and attitudes formed throughout adolescence can be quite long-lasting, it is preferable for the youngster to have every physical and psychological advantage as he reaches that age. In one study, for example, slender adult women who had been overweight as children or adolescents were asked how they perceived themselves.

Surprisingly, only those women who were overweight in adolescence suffered psychological consequences and continued to consider themselves as unattractive as adults. Attitudes formed throughout their adolescence have remained with them. We hope the relevance for ADHD youngsters is evident. The sooner maladaptive learning can be avoided, the better because the child will have fewer problems in adolescence and later in life.

However, if such habits or attitudes are developed, the future is not bleak. Learned habits can be unlearned, skills can be acquired, and new experiences can affect a person's personality during the course of their life. In subsequent chapters, we shall look at several psychological techniques that are relevant here. However, based on our knowledge of children's growth and development, early treatment appears to be more successful than later treatment.

When ADHD symptoms remain to a large extent throughout adolescence, special concerns arise because the ADHD issues interact with normal psychological changes that occur during puberty. Peers play an increasingly important part in children's social development as they get older. As youngsters enter puberty, the influence of their peers is even stronger. Parents may become distressed when they discover that their adolescent child has adopted peer group values that contradict previously approved household values. The adolescent is eager to establish intimate relationships with his peers. Closeness with peers takes the role of closeness with parents. Adolescents confide in one another yet frequently mumble or remain silent with their parents.

However, developing relationships with classmates might be difficult for the preadolescent ADHD youngster. Peer difficulties persist for the ADHD adolescent who continues to lack social perceptiveness and interpersonal abilities. If his ADHD impairments interfere with the kinds of talents that make adolescents popular, such as poor coordination in sports performance, he is also limited in acquiring close friends. Peer rejection is significantly more hurtful in puberty than it is in childhood.

Some ADHD youngsters appear to derive less enjoyment from activities that other children love. They may need excitement and risk to feel the joy that other youngsters get from less stimulating activities. The drive for excitement, combined with ongoing poor self-esteem (exacerbated by peer rejection), impaired social skills, and impulsivity, increases the likelihood that the ADHD adolescent would associate with delinquent friends.

The development of autonomy—feelings of self-sufficiency and emancipation from one's parents—is an important area of psychological maturation in teenagers. This is a healthy trend, even if it produces some tension between parents and adolescents. The degree of the disagreement may be determined by how the adolescent exhibits his or her growing autonomy. Preferences for current adolescent fashions in music, hairstyles, and clothing may irritate parents mildly, but taking idealistic or activist political opinions that differ from parental ones, or becoming a member of a social outgroup, can result in the major breakdown of family bonds.

Establishing sexual connections is another crucial teenage developmental activity that demands social ease and social abilities. The ADHD adolescent may not be shy as a result of his social ineptitude, but he may be inefficient in sexual relationships as a result of his social ineptitude. Several studies, on the other hand, have found that ADHD youth are developing a pattern of early sexual activity, more casual sex and sexual partners, and are more likely to have a sexually transmitted disease that can subsequently progress into adulthood.

Another issue that persists in those who have an insufficient conscience as youngsters is a lack of self-control. Self-control entails numerous psychological characteristics that ADHD teenagers tend to lack: impulse control, empathy, and the ability to perceive one's effect on others. These deficiencies are typical of social immaturity and enhance the likelihood that the ADHD adolescent would engage in delinquent behavior. Indeed, comprehensive research has revealed that ADHD youngsters are substantially more prone than their non-ADHD classmates to develop alcohol and drug misuse issues, have serious accidents, and engage in antisocial conduct during adolescence. These trials included untreated ADHD teenagers, as well as individuals with undiagnosed conduct disorder who are chronic rule-breakers.

LONGITUDINAL STUDIES

Longitudinal studies, the other way to determine changes in ADHD over time discussed previously, have proven very helpful in understanding what happens in adulthood. The longest of these lasted thirty-three years and delivered information about ADHD to people in their forties. Several other shorter-term studies of this type have lately been conducted in Montreal, Milwaukee, Pittsburgh, and Chicago. We are establishing an understanding of what happens to ADHD as people age by combining the findings from all of our research.

The most well-known, largest, and longest study was conducted in New York City. Approximately 200 children with ADHD but neither ODD nor CD, as well as a matching sample of non-ADHD boys, who were first examined between the ages of six and twelve, were reinterviewed at an average of eighteen, twenty-six, and forty-one. Researchers discovered that at the age of eighteen, 40% of the original ADHD youngsters still had serious issues with ADHD symptoms; however, at the age of forty-one, it was 22%.

In addition, the study found that ADHD patients "had significantly worse educational, occupational, economic, and social outcomes, as well as more divorces than comparisons." These estimates probably certainly underestimate the children's difficulties' persistence. For example, the persistence of ADHD into a person's early twenties is considerably more likely to be in the neighborhood of 50% of children than the study's lower percentage. The investigators relied solely on the children's descriptions of their symptoms; they did not interview their parents. We know that ADHD children of all ages, as well as ADHD adults, underestimate the scope and severity of their issues. When we interview adults with suspected ADHD parents — as well as the adults' partners — we discover that a substantially higher proportion of them report having problems than the patients do.

This is most likely an understatement because they did not interview parents or other informants, and we know from our clinical work with ADHD adults that many patients see their ADHD difficulties as mild or minor while their partners see them as moderate to severe.

After an average of thirty-three years in the study, people who had ADHD as children showed many differences as adults, including three times as many incarcerations, three times as many divorces, three times as much drug and cigarette use, four times as many psychiatric hospitalizations, very little higher education, and a $40,000 lower annual salary. Two other significant findings were that ADHD children of all ages were substantially more likely to develop issues with conduct (oppositional defiant disorder and the more severe conduct disorder) and substance misuse, although having neither when they entered the study. Worryingly, they had a significantly higher risk of developing antisocial personality disorder, an adult version of a particularly severe form of conduct disorder and criminality.

The association between ADHD and substance misuse in adulthood is unclear; some alcoholic reports have indicated that while ADHD youth are more likely to use alcohol, they are also more prone to use other substances. However, several of these findings did not differentiate between children with "pure" ADHD and those with a combination of ADHD and behavioral issues. Children with a combination of ADHD and behavioral disorders are more likely to abuse alcohol. In practice, around one-quarter of ADHD children have an alcoholic parent.

One crucial aspect of these longitudinal investigations should not be overlooked. The children who took part in the study either did not receive or continued to receive medication, therapy, or remedial education.

These studies only show what will happen if ADHD children do not receive ongoing therapy. So, what are the outcomes? They are three in number. First, ADHD is likely to continue to cause significant issues in one-third to two-thirds of adults. Second, ADHD children are far more susceptible than normal children to conduct disorder, especially if they have an oppositional defiant disorder. Third, ADHD children are more prone to acquire alcohol and other substance misuse issues in adolescence, possibly only if they have conduct disorder.

These findings may be discouraging. However, early and well-managed medical treatment combined with well-managed psychological treatment may prevent – or considerably minimize – the psychological symptoms that occur as a result of physiological abnormalities. Of course, such treatment does not heal the underlying physiological problems, and it is possible that some previous treatment programs were ineffectual because they did not continue to deliver medication as long as ADHD symptoms persisted. The number of children who continue to have issues despite treatment is higher than previously thought. Because we now have evidence that many ADHD children continue to have the same physiological difficulties in adulthood (inattention, hot temper, inability to complete tasks, and so on) and respond to medication, it appears obvious that some ADHD children may benefit from — and may need to take — medication for many years after childhood. Can such treatment help children avoid ADHD problems or deal with them more effectively? The answer appears to be a cautious "yes," albeit more research is needed.

ADHD researchers have recently discovered that in a high number of cases, ADHD difficulties remain in one's thirties, forties, and fifties. And, in recent years, the identification of ADHD in adults has skyrocketed (and, most likely, has been overdiagnosed).

We initially became aware of ADHD in adults when speaking with parents of ADHD children. Parents generally acknowledged being inattentive and hyperactive as children, and many claimed that while some of their difficulties had lessened with age, they still plagued them to an aggravating degree. These adults varied from ADHD children not just in that some of their difficulties were less severe but also in that they had established adult coping mechanisms. Our revelation that many adults who continued to suffer from ADHD difficulties could benefit from medication treatment just as much as ADHD youngsters were of great curiosity and practical value.

Similarly, learning disabilities might last well into one's thirties and forties. Learning-disordered children tend to lag further and further behind as they become older. A significant proportion of learning-disordered children have substantial issues long into adulthood. Others show some improvement, but learning-disordered youngsters are generally slow readers and poor spellers, and if they have difficulty with arithmetic, they continue to struggle with mathematical computations.

How can we effectively summarize what we've learned thus far? How often does ADHD remain into adulthood? The most conservative estimate appears to be between one-third and two-thirds. The intensity varies greatly, from modest symptoms of inattention and disorganization — and possibly restlessness — to individuals who have persistent childhood problems that may have changed shape with adulthood.

At this point, the best estimate is that roughly half have major symptoms and unfavorable outcomes, one-quarter have moderate symptoms, and one-quarter have limited symptoms or none at all; however, different scientists come up with different percentages.

Chapter 7
Adhd In Adults

WHAT IS ADULT ADHD?

Adult Attention Deficit Hyperactivity Disorder (ADHD) is a condition that affects 60% of adults who have ADHD as a child. ADHD is a complicated neurological and behavioral illness that causes inattention, erratic and impulsive conduct, and the inability to complete activities. ADHD patients are usually irritable, impatient, and have poor or non-existent organizational abilities.

ADHD appears exclusively in childhood. Adults do not develop the disorder. Adults with ADHD may not have been diagnosed as children, and an examination into his or her past may help confirm a diagnosis. A history of low academic achievement and frequent disciplinary charges may indicate ADHD. Children with ADHD frequently have to repeat one or more grade levels and have a higher total dropout rate. If possible, interviewing the adult patient's parents is an effective strategy to acquire data to support an ADHD diagnosis.

Adults with ADHD may experience minor symptoms, allowing them to effectively deal and work around concerns such as the inability to concentrate. Patients with a mild form of the condition may struggle to complete everyday tasks, but they have no trouble keeping concentrated on activities that are of great interest to them. Patients who have minor symptoms may be able to regulate their urges more easily. When an inclination of anger or irritation arises, for example, an individual may be able to build a habit of deep breathing and counting to 15.

Adults with severe ADHD have a far more difficult time dealing with symptoms on their own. Concentration and task completion will remain challenging regardless of how intriguing or entertaining the activity is. Frustration frequently results in destructive conduct and bad or nonexistent relationships.

Adults suffering from the illness frequently struggle to maintain intimate ties. Patients with ADHD have a high divorce rate and frequently have many marriages. Due to an inability to regulate impulses and angry outbursts, the patient's relationships frequently suffer. Difficulties in completing tasks may disturb relationships, leading to more strife.

Another area where persons with ADHD struggle is job stability and performance. Inability to remember assignments frequently leads to missing meetings and deadlines. Work tasks are frequently not finished because the adult travels from one task to another without completing the original assignment. Patients with ADHD have poor organizational skills or none at all, resulting in delayed and poor job performance. Uncontrolled outbursts of rage, combined with a low threshold for annoyance and impatience, can generate issues with coworkers. ADHD patients frequently change jobs, have limited work skills, and have a bad employment history.

Multiple social issues frequently affect the adult patient who also has ADHD. The inability to excel at work and maintain a job frequently maintains an individual in a lower socioeconomic class. Difficulties controlling one's temper, as well as having higher levels of impatience and a lower threshold for irritation, are frequently exhibited adversely on the road. Adults with ADHD are prone to multiple driving offenses, which result in fines, suspensions, and accidents. Driving issues exacerbate the individual's issues by making it difficult to get to work due to suspensions and higher debt due to court fines and increased insurance prices.

In adults with ADHD, social maladjustment frequently leads to substance abuse. Patients are more likely to smoke cigarettes and seek relief from mental distress through substance usage. ADHD sufferers frequently utilize alcohol and illegal drugs to escape the emotional discomfort produced by their condition. Being impaired frequently allows ADHD patients to feel more at ease in social situations by providing them with a false sense of confidence.

ADHD treatments include medication, behavior modification, or a combination of the two. Several drugs that are successful in treating ADHD symptoms are available via prescription. Surprisingly, despite the fact that hyperactivity is a component of the disorder, stimulants are used to treat the condition and create a soothing effect. Even though stimulants are effective at controlling ADHD symptoms, the nature of the disorder makes medication use a sometimes risky option. Patients with ADHD are frequently prone to substance abuse, and stimulants are controlled substances that are frequently taken illegally. In ADHD patients, forgetfulness and a lack of organization frequently lead to overmedicating or undermedicating.

Adults with ADHD can also benefit from effective behavioral therapy. Goals for impulse and anger management, as well as routines to aid attention and organization, are gradually adopted. Individuals with ADHD should be exposed to new skills and habits gradually to avoid the beginning of frustration. Individually introduced new habits are more likely to be mastered and established. Psychological therapy is also initiated to assist the patient in developing a more positive self-image and establishing confidence. Higher self-esteem leads to confidence, which allows the patient to cultivate healthy connections and take satisfaction in work and other accomplishments.

Patients taking ADHD therapy should have their progress checked on a regular basis. Improvements and alterations in symptoms will necessitate changes in treatment and goals. Individuals with ADHD who are properly diagnosed can alleviate their suffering and lead healthier lives with more positive relationships and personal success.

SIGNS AND SYMPTOMS OF ADHD IN ADULTS

If you know someone well, you can usually identify if they have ADHD by seeing certain characteristics or symptoms.

Here is a simple checklist to assist you in identifying an adult with ADHD:

- They are often late for work appointments and social engagements.
- They are impulsive.
- They are disorganized.
- They find it hard to complete tasks on time.
- They are a chronic procrastinator.
- They drive recklessly or ignore traffic rules.
- They cannot focus or concentrate on one thing for long.

- They are restless.
- They become frustrated easily.
- They have frequent mood swings and often become angry or irritated very quickly.
- They have a low tolerance for stress.
- They have unstable relationships.
- They have low self-esteem.

Many people are guilty of one, two, or even all of the items on the list above. It does not automatically imply that they have ADHD. However, there is cause for concern if a person possesses three-fourths or more of the qualities listed. If they did and were diagnosed with ADHD as a child, they are likely to have ADHD as an adult as well. The same conclusion applies even if they were not diagnosed with childhood ADHD, but their parents or instructors assumed they did.

All people with ADHD had it as children, according to mental health doctors, even if it was never recognized. According to statistics, up to 40% of children with ADHD will continue to have the mental disease when they reach adulthood. Some of these adults may now have fewer or milder symptoms than when they were children. Others may continue to exhibit clear symptoms, causing substantial difficulty in some areas of their life, including their profession and relationships.

In the sections that follow, we'll take a closer look at the most common symptoms of ADHD in adults.

ADHD risk factors

Adult ADHD is more likely if any of the following conditions exist:

- They have a parent, sibling or any blood relative who has ADHD or another mental disorder (such as depression, anxiety or bipolar disorder).
- Their mother, while pregnant with them, smoked, used drugs or drank alcohol.
- During their mother's pregnancy with them, she was exposed to environmental poisons such as polychlorinated biphenyls or PCBs.
- When they were a child, they were exposed to environmental toxins, such as lead (in the paint on toys) and in old pipes.
- They had a premature birth.

General symptoms of ADHD in adults

The most common symptoms seen in adults with ADHD are:

- Difficulty concentrating and sustaining focus
- Trouble with prioritizing activities or planning
- Disorganization and messiness
- Forgetfulness and constantly losing things
- Impatience or restlessness
- Impulsivity
- Chronic lateness for work and important events
- Being easily distracted
- Lack of self-control (which includes the inability to control impulses, anger, and rude or inappropriate behavior)
- Being easily bored when doing dull or routine activities
- Selective hyperfocus, or the ability to focus intently on something that they find enjoyable or interesting
- Low tolerance for stress and frustration
- Low self-esteem, insecurity and feelings of inferiority or under-achievement

These symptoms have unintended effects. Frequently, the unfavorable consequences of certain symptoms include:

- Missed deadlines and non-completion of tasks started
- Forgetting to attend meetings or show up for social engagements
- Poor job performance (or poor academic performance if the person is in school)
- Inability to hold down a job for long
- Stress-induced anxiety or depression
- Mood swings and quick bursts of anger – These are often the result of feeling restless, bored or impatient, such as when waiting in line and driving in heavy traffic.
- Unstable relationships – Problems arise when those around the person with ADHD constantly nag them to be more tidy or organized and when they become hurt and resentful of the person's behavior to the point that they perceive it to be insensitive and irresponsible.
- Awkwardness in social settings
- Trouble with the law
- Substance abuse (alcohol or drugs)
- Financial problems (due mainly to the lack of a steady job and impulsive spending)
- Physical health issues (may be due to compulsive eating, substance abuse, skipping doctor's appointments and forgetting to take important medications)
- Mental health problems (brought about by chronic stress, anxiety and low self-esteem)
- Frequent accidents (especially vehicular mishaps)

Of course, experiencing these symptoms and their effects is not enough to demonstrate the diagnosis of ADHD. Only a registered mental health professional's expert diagnosis can achieve that.

ADHD must be diagnosed carefully because it is readily confused with other psychological diseases or mental disorders. Furthermore, ADHD frequently coexists with various other psychiatric disorders, occurring at the same time and in the same person. Other psychological conditions are as follows:

- Learning disabilities are seen in people who perform poorly in school and who score very low for their age on academic and intelligence tests.
- Personality disorders, including antisocial and borderline personality disorders
- Mood disorders such as depression and bipolar (manic-depressive) disorder
- Anxiety disorders such as panic, obsessive-compulsive and social anxiety disorders

NOTE: Given that ADHD can be confused with any of these diseases and that it can exist concurrently with them, it is critical that anyone suspected of having ADHD seek professional diagnosis and treatment as soon as possible. An excellent starting point for them would be to see their family doctor. Following that, the doctor may recommend them to a good mental health specialist (a psychologist or a psychiatrist) for more testing.

Hello from the Author,

As you embark on this journey of truly understanding Adhd, I would like to request a small gesture that holds immeasurable value to me as an author.

Your genuine feedback is a beacon of encouragement for me, as it reinforces the belief that my words have made a meaningful impact on you, and really helps me out as a small author. Your words are not only a testament to your own experience but also a guiding light for those who are considering embarking on this journey themselves.

To leave feedback on Amazon, simply navigate to the book's page and click on the "Write a Customer Review" button.

Thank you; now let's get back to the book.

David Whitehead

Chapter 8
Step 1: Establish Rules

There is substantial evidence that certain approaches to dealing with ADHD youngsters are more effective than others. It has been discovered that the optimal home environment is one that is firm, constant, explicit, and predictable. Let me explain the significance of these concepts in the context of ADHD child discipline.

Firm: Firms imply that the child's rules or expectations always have the same consequences. If somebody violates a certain rule, he is always penalized in the same way. When he does what is expected of him, he is always acknowledged or praised.

Consistent: Consistent indicates that the regulations themselves do not alter from day to day. If he is expected to tidy up his room before going out to play, he will never leave it until it is spotless.

Explicit: Explicit indicates that everything is clearly specified and understood by all parties. For example, "cleaned up" could mean that clothing was hanging in the closet, the bed was made, toys were returned to a shelf, the room was vacuumed and dusted, or any combination of these. The definition of cleaning up for the cleaning-up rule must be specific enough so that both the child and the parents understand the regulation.

Predictable: Predictable laws are those that are enacted before, rather than after, a crime occurs. Naturally, all parental expectations for the child cannot be conveyed in advance. Parents never think about warning their toddler not to put nail paint on the rug, and they even less often think about asking him not to put a toy car in his ear. Some things can only be dealt with after they occur. In general, rules may and should be established and enforced for most daily tasks. Every day, the child must wash himself, brush his teeth, and perform his housework and homework; regulations governing these basic duties should be created.

Enforcement of these rules, such as removing him from the setting or removing distracting items, should follow any infraction but should not be used if the rules have not been agreed upon beforehand. The speed restrictions for driving have analogous regular and predictable standards for adults.

It is easier to follow a precise speed restriction, like 55 mph, than it is to follow the ambiguous limit of "reasonable and proper," as it was previously called in some Western states. When there is a hazy speed restriction, it is impossible to discern how fast one can go if it is twilight and light rain is pouring. Someone who is afraid may drive at 35 mph. Someone who is more daring and drives at 40 mph may be rightfully furious if she receives a ticket.

These proposals may appear severe and potentially cruel to parents. They may also appear to contradict various benign permissive beliefs that promote letting children "do their own things" and providing opportunities for parents and children to discuss issues. Let us clear up some frequent misunderstandings. To begin with, firmness is not the same as harshness.

Harshness is defined as harsh or cruel rule enforcement. To imprison someone for life for driving too fast is harsh. Every time he does this, he will be fined. Second, kids require structure. They require defined standards, expectations, and values to live by. Such structure does not imply a lack of freedom.

If a community is to function well, its members must adhere to specific rules and expectations. Adults must not steal, drive while intoxicated, or embezzle. They are not permitted to urinate in public. Following such principles benefits the individual as well. For starters, it keeps him out of trouble. However, it also directly benefits some people. Someone who has only recently learned to control his urges must expend a significant amount of energy simply controlling himself. The reformed alcoholic or drug addict must put out considerable effort to avoid relapse. A person who has learned to easily manage himself has energies that he can use usefully elsewhere.

This is not in conflict with self-expression or creativity. A clever person who is unable to focus his energies will not be productive (remember the ancient adage that brilliance is one percent inspiration and ninety-nine percent perspiration).

Firm, consistent standards for behavior have nothing to do with the child's self-expression or parental-child understanding. We've been discussing behavioral rules, not mental and emotional rules. Thoughts and feelings are not the same as conduct. They cannot be controlled, and the parent should not seek to control them. As we will see later, parents should assist their children in acknowledging and expressing their emotions. However, both the parent and the child must always distinguish between feelings and conduct. Parents of an ADHD child, for example, should allow him to express his jealousy toward his newborn sister, but he should not be permitted to hurt her. Feeling envious and punching out of envy are as diametrically opposed as night and day.

Finally, establishing clear standards should not interfere with constructive dialogue between parents and children. Such chats should undoubtedly become a part of family life as the child grows older, but they may also be beneficial when he is younger. For example, the youngster may offer ways to complete the tasks that he prefers and that do not jeopardize the family's safety. This is very appropriate and should be promoted. However, deliberation should not preclude regulations from being developed. It may have an impact on how they are decided, and it may change their exact parameters, but it should not prevent them from being established publicly and consistently.

What evidence exists that the type of structure suggested here is beneficial? Research conducted in the mid-1930s with highly "hyperactive" children yielded some very interesting results. These children's behavior was so out of control at home that they were admitted to a hospital for children with serious behavioral issues.

The doctors had no prior experience with such children and tried a variety of procedures to see which would be most helpful. They began by believing that the children's problems were the consequence of excessive emotional stress and strain, and they treated them as such. This strategy caused a temporary period of improvement, which was quickly followed by the reappearance of the same behavioral difficulties.

The children were then treated in individual psychotherapy because they had never had psychotherapy before. This technique was also unsuccessful. Finally, the doctors resolved to foster an environment that was "constructive," "restrictive," and "tolerant." The rules were not lax, and the youngsters were expected to follow them strictly. Children were isolated but not chastised for their impulsive conduct, and once they calmed down, they were assisted in expressing themselves.

The final treatment definitely provided the greatest benefit, and many children were able to be discharged from the hospital and returned to their families. Unfortunately, children who returned to homes where their parents were unable to be firm were frequently disturbed and had to return to the hospital. It is crucial to note that not all children benefited from this (or any other) strategy, but it was the most effective.

This and comparable research provide evidence that organized surroundings can aid ADHD children. There is also evidence that they are most beneficial when started early in life and are ineffective (perhaps useless) when started later in infancy. The approaches that will be discussed may be quite beneficial to a preschool or young school-aged youngster. They may be less successful with an ADHD youngster reaching puberty.

What the specific regulations should be in a given family are determined by parental preferences and the child's age. In theory, parents might set any rules they want and teach their children to follow them. (Different cultures have radically different laws and standards for child conduct, and each culture strives to produce a "standard product," a child who is well acclimated to life in that society.) The parents' leeway in establishing these guidelines lessens as the child grows older. Most of the time, the young youngster is solely aware of how his own family operates. The older child is well aware of how other children and their families conduct themselves and will rebel if his parents' standards appear to be different. A mother can maintain her two-year-old son's hair in long curls, and he will not object.

But she'd be crazy to try to give her fourteen-year-old a prep-school haircut if his buddies all look like the latest rock idol. The earlier a child is taught rules and values, the more likely he is to follow them later in life, especially in the face of divergent standards outside the family.

The approaches to be discussed are more effective on younger children, say, those under the age of 10 or eleven. These tactics, which require the child to remain dependent and controlled by his parents, are not appropriate for teenagers; they demand a different psychological approach.

The first duty for parents with younger children is to decide concretely and clearly which behaviors demand limitations or adjustment. It is critical to be concrete and particular in order for the regulations to be presented clearly and unambiguously. Let us look at some examples of ambiguous, meaningless rules and how to clarify them.

1. "He should clean his room." As previously stated, this regulation is exceedingly unclear. If the parent means "cleaning the room," and the youngster understands "make your bed," he may feel aggrieved if he makes his bed, departs, and is chastised. Furthermore, there is plenty of opportunity for dispute. The boy cleaned the room according to his standards but not according to his mother's. We will return to this subject later in the section labeled "Chores."

2. "He should have better table manners." This could imply that he should eat with a fork rather than his fingers, that he should place a napkin on his lap, that he should say "please,"; and that he should not use a boardinghouse reach.

3. "He should treat his little sister better." This could suggest that he should not beat her, that he should let her play with his toys, and that he should not retaliate when she hits him.

4. "He should be neater." This could mean tying his shoelaces, buttoning his shirt, washing his face, and brushing his teeth.

Not only does the youngster not understand what his parents mean if they are not specific—and he may and will fight with them in the best legalistic fashion about what they could have meant—but parents will also have a far more difficult time judging whether improvement has occurred.

The second responsibility of parents is to build a rule hierarchy of priority. They must determine what is vital, significant, nice, and trivial. The parents must determine which rules are five stars and which are one star. They must tailor the punishment to the crime and differentiate between felonies and misdemeanors.

They cannot, in effect, punish unlawful parking with life in prison and murder with a warning.

Parents, for example, have been known to employ a lecture as punishment for starting a serious fire and a violent thrashing as punishment for bad assignment performance. The use of five- and one-star guidelines allows parents to focus on the most crucial areas first, giving the youngster some breathing room. After the primary issues have been resolved, the parents can proceed to the next category.

Another job for the parents is to decide ahead of time that both mother and father would follow the prescribed course of action. This policy is not always simple to implement. Frequently, each parent has developed his or her own (usually unsuccessful) method of dealing with the child, and unfortunately, each frequently believes that his or her method is correct and that the child's issues are the consequence of the other's mismanagement.

If such a family environment exists, it contradicts the continuous united front that is a must for helping the ADHD youngster learn to manage his behavior. It is not necessary for the parents to agree; they must merely operate in concert. If parents are unable to resolve their disagreements and reach an agreement on rules and standards for their ADHD child's behavior, they may benefit from psychological counseling. A psychiatrist, social worker, or psychologist may be able to help them sort out these distinctions and identify the set of rules, as well as the relative relevance of the various rules, that are required for their ADHD child.

Chapter 9
Step 2: Establish Rewards And Punishments

In addition to establishing sound rules to assist the child, parents must design a system of rewards and punishments ahead of time. These rewards and punishments must be perceived as such by the youngster, not just the parents. Some people associate the phrases "reward" and "punishment" with negative connotations. "Reward" suggests bribery, whereas "punishment" implies harshness. The term "reward" simply refers to something the child enjoys, such as attention, praise, or a modest special pleasure. Certain privileges, toys, and so on can be beneficial under certain circumstances, which will be explained later.

Similarly, punishment simply refers to something the child dislikes. It does not imply long-term violence, emotional neglect, or deprivation of privileges. In general, using "time-out," such as sending the child to his room until he stops behaving in an unwanted way (e.g., having a tantrum) or performing a required job (e.g., getting dressed), is the most effective and non-harmful punishment with younger children. It is more beneficial to say, "Please go to your room and return to breakfast when your shoes are tied and your face is washed," than to yell at or spank the youngster.

There are two additional essential reward and punishment principles. To begin, in order to be most effective, a reward or punishment should be immediate. Any lag reduces effectiveness. When a youngster does what you want him to do, immediately praise him. If he does something he has been taught not to do, discipline him immediately. Do not make long-distance offers ("any toy you want two weeks from now") or threats of punishment ("Daddy will spank you when he gets home"). Second, the once-only rule should be implemented. Parents should develop the practice of saying do or don't only once before rewarding or punishing their children. If they do not follow this guideline, if they do not give their children the first, second, third, and tenth warnings before acting, their children will learn to commit ten offenses before becoming concerned.

Meanwhile, the parents will have gotten sore throats and accumulated a lot of rage. In certain circumstances, the child may have pushed his parents to take a stand. Surprisingly, when the parent eventually acts, most youngsters are relieved. The application of this one-time rule can save a lot of trouble.

Animal experiments have taught psychologists a lot about reward and punishment over the last sixty years.

Researchers have discovered relatively easy and effective strategies for teaching animals such as pigeons and rats to complete extremely complex tasks. Since then, psychologists have discovered that such techniques, known as "operant conditioning" or behavior modification, can be useful in teaching and controlling the behaviors of humans whose psychological difficulties are so severe that they previously appeared unreachable by any known technique—for example, profoundly retarded children and adults, children of normal intelligence who are unable to speak, and severely disturbed adult psychiatric patients. In recent years, several psychologists have attempted to adapt these "operant" strategies to youngsters with behavioral issues. The operant techniques—or operant conditioning—are simply refined sets of rewards and punishments, and the psychologists' work can be translated into recommendations that can be very useful to parents of ADHD children.

Although the precise rules and regulations of operant conditioning utilized in the laboratory are rather difficult, the underlying premise that parents can use is really easy. Their repercussions have an impact on actions. That is, what happens after an animal or youngster does something strongly increases the likelihood of him doing the same thing again, either favorably or adversely. This means that how parents react when their child does or says anything will either enhance or lessen the likelihood that the youngster will repeat the behavior.

This notion is best illustrated by using operant training, specifically "reinforcement," with animals. A typical demonstration in an introductory psychology course will be described. A cage holds a hungry pigeon. The experimenter stands outside the cage, looking through a one-way screen at the pigeon. He has a switch in his hand that he can use to make a click in the box and deliver a kernel of corn to the pigeon in a feeding dish. The experimenter may force the pigeon to execute any activity that pigeons are capable of. In one case, it was decided to have the pigeon spin counterclockwise, like a ballerina.

To accomplish this, the scientist waited until the pigeon had turned slightly to the left during his typical wanderings. The experimenter pressed the switch after the pigeon had done so, and the pigeon received a kernel of grain. The pigeon turned to the left again in the next twenty or thirty seconds, and the experimenter administered another kernel of corn. Within a few minutes, the pigeon began to rotate slightly to the left. After a while, the experimenter returned with another kernel of corn. The pigeon began to turn in a circle continually for the following five or ten minutes. The experimenter would wait until the bird was turning quickly before delivering the food. The class was astounded to see a pigeon revolving like a whirling dervish at the end of the half-hour. This experiment demonstrates how complex tasks may be taught to animals. More complicated behavior can be taught to humans, and (as animal trials cannot demonstrate) such learning can occur without the person's consciousness as well as with his awareness.

Before delving into the subject of how relevant this experiment is for humans, let us first define two concepts from operant conditioning therapy. The first of these terms is "operant," while the second is "reinforcement." An operant is any voluntary act that an animal or person can execute. It includes the circling of the pigeon. In reality, it encompasses the majority of behaviors. It may even involve talking, getting attention, throwing tantrums, waking up in the middle of the night, lying, stealing, sobbing, starting fires, writing poems, or philosophizing—in short, virtually anything. The term "reinforcement" is equivalent to "reward." Food was used as reinforcement in the animal experiment. A hungry animal finds food pleasurable or encouraging.

What do youngsters find reinforcing? That is dependent on their current situation. Food is no longer rewarding to the rat who has had his fill, and he will not depress a bar to receive it. Water can be reinforcing to a thirsty youngster; food can be reinforcing to a hungry child. However, most of the child's actions are impacted by parental conduct that is significantly distinct from simple hunger or thirst satisfaction. Reinforcing behavior varies depending on the child; however, some parental acts and behaviors are reinforcing to practically all children. As previously said, parental attachment and parental attention are the most vital.

Parental attention is most likely the most common reinforcer in a child's life. It is significant not just because it is frequently directed towards the child but also because it is reinforcing regardless of what generates it. As a result, some forms of punishment are more rewarding to a child than ignoring him. Expressing displeasure with a child's most recent misbehavior is giving him attention. Thus, ironically, the risk of a child repeating a misdeed may be raised when the parent discusses the misdeed with the child for an extended period of time.

What about harsher punishment? Psychologists refer to the reinforcers we've covered as positive reinforcers. What the ordinary calls punishment, the psychologist refers to it as negative reinforcement. Certain broad rules about the impacts and efficiency of negative reinforcement have been discovered.

First, negative reinforcement diminishes the likelihood of the preceding behavior being repeated. As generations of parents have discovered, a "good spanking" was a reasonably effective technique of deterring a child from doing what he just did that the parents didn't like with most children, most of the time. The rat which received a powerful electric shock after pressing the bar will not do it again, or at least not in the near future.

Psychologists have also discovered some less visible aspects of punishment. If the punishment is severe (e.g., a painful electric shock that is nearly enough to paralyze the animal), the animal is unlikely to repeat the behavior, but punishments of this type are also likely to be followed with side effects that modify the animal in a variety of negative ways. Animals subjected to such severe penalties can become erratic and frequently exhibit disturbed (neurotic) behavior in other areas. Electric shocks were used to educate dogs to avoid items in experiments, and the dogs became violent, exuberant, withdrawn, or highly scared. In other words, the punishment that is effective enough to permanently prevent offensive behavior may induce more troubling behavior than it prevents.

As a result, some punishment draws attention to the child, reinforcing poor behavior, and severe punishment is likely to have negative side effects; hence, the question arises as to whether any form of punishment can be reasonably effective. Although psychologists differ, it appears that milder forms of punishment can temporarily reduce behavior. That is, shocks that do not cause the animal to become neurotic are unlikely to be effective for long. The significance of this for youngsters should be self-evident. Humane parents apply only modest discipline, and the effects of punishment should not be expected to persist long in ADHD children, who are typically not particularly susceptible to punishment. In fact, they are infrequently.

Positive reinforcement, on the other hand, may not be permanent, but certain changes may be exceptionally long-lasting. Its advantage is that once the child is on the proper course, he will most likely receive reinforcement from persons other than his family. The youngster who is trained to be relatively courteous and who is helped by medicine to be moderately obedient and moderately non-aggressive will be encouraged by positive attention from others, gaining friends, and succeeding.

Another strategy for extending the benefits of positive reinforcement is to gradually reduce the frequency and predictability of the reinforcement. To begin, reinforce a child whenever he does the desired behavior. After a while, the payout is changed, and he is gradually reinforced less frequently for the same behavior. The child is now more inclined to continue this behavior in the absence of a consistent payoff.

After criticizing punishment (not for humane reasons, but for practical ones), we must concede that it has some effectiveness and can be useful in dangerous or life-threatening situations. The two-year-old who runs out into the street (perhaps to his death) must be dealt with firmly and swiftly. This will reduce the risk of him repeating the act in the near future. However, keeping him out of the street is more likely if he is positively reinforced for doing activities that deter him from getting there (e.g., staying on the lawn or playing in the backyard). Punishment may be a helpful short-term strategy, but it is useless in the long run for most ADHD youngsters. Even when punishment is essential (as in the case of the two-year-old stated above), it should be as mild and as infrequently employed as feasible.

One issue that we have touched on but must highlight is the timing of reinforcement. One word sums it up: immediately. The technique's success in animal tests is dependent on the animal receiving reinforcement immediately after the act— the operant — is accomplished. A two-second delay lessens its effectiveness slightly, a five-second delay significantly reduces it, and a minute delay renders it worthless. Although children appear to be able to withstand longer waits, the same concept applies to them.

Positive reinforcement (or reward) and negative reinforcement (or punishment) are far more effective when given right away. If a child does what his parent wants him to do, he should be praised right away.

If he commits something that necessitates punishment, he should be disciplined right away. Promising a youngster a reward in two weeks if he gets good grades now or delaying required chastise-ment till Daddy gets home is unproductive and a waste of time. Such reinforcements will only operate temporarily and will have no long-term effect.

The topic of how these strategies should be applied to children emerges from this discussion. They can be used both casually and formally. Clearly, a key aspect of its informal implementa-tion is that children should be instantly positively encouraged when they perform what their parents wish. When the child understands what his parents want (for example, putting his shoes away, eating with a fork, saying "please"), he should be reinforced in a specific way every time he does these activities. By "specific," we mean that the parents should make believable and relevant comments about the desired conduct. If he is requested to put his shoes away and does so, he should not be told, "You are a wonderful son." "I am very pleased that you are learning to take care of your things like a grown-up boy," or words to that effect should be said by the parent.

Children, like adults, identify exaggerated praise as deceptive. The child should understand why he is being praised. In theory, the comparable concept to be implemented when children behave inappropriately would necessitate that the children be ignored; yet, how can the parent overlook undesired behavior? It is simple if the child is dressed like a clown. Ignoring him is risky or expensive if he is pummeling his three-year-old sister or wrecking the house. Ignoring him is simple if he is engaging in harmless attention-seeking behavior. Ignoring should be supplemented with the isolation room or time-out strategy if he is engaging in destructive or damaging activity.

When one considers what normally happens when a youngster misbehaves, the utility of time-out becomes clear. For example, if a youngster punches his sister, the parent should, at the very least, ask, "Why did you do that?" As a result, the child gets attention for misbehaving. According to the ideas mentioned, paying attention increases the likelihood that the youngster would repeat the behavior.

In other words, the normal conversation between the parents and the child is likely to result in increased future misbehavior. When using the time-out technique, the youngster is notified ahead of time that he will be taken to his room if he misbehaves. When he misbehaves, he is simply told that he is going to his room and will be able to return as soon as he regains control. That is great if he goes freely. If he has to be carried, it is not ideal, but it is effective.

If he tries to escape his room, a screen door latch should be installed and fastened outside the door. When the youngster calms down, or, in the case of the older child, when he says that he has calmed down and comes out himself, the parent sits down with the child and discusses what was bothering him previously. This strategy rewards the child for being in control of himself rather than for being out of control. After a youngster has had a lot of practice with this technique, he will frequently learn to go to his room when he is sad and come out when he is no longer upset. If the child must be held in the room, the parents should not allow him to go until he has regained control of himself, his tantrum has ended, or his angry outburst has subsided.

This strategy has been utilized successfully with both severely disturbed inpatient psychiatric patients and ADHD children. It is particularly useful with younger (under the age of nine or ten) ADHD youngsters.

The second kind of reinforcement therapy, the more formal method, cannot be utilized with the youngest ADHD children, but it is successful with children over the age of six. This strategy allows the parent and child to pick which tasks the child should complete. These could be tasks that happen every day or once a week. They could include things like making his bed, putting his clothing in the hamper, or taking out the garbage. A weekly chart is maintained, and the parent and child agree on how many tokens, such as poker chips, the child will earn for doing as agreed.

When the child completes the assignment, he is given the prede-termined quantity of poker chips. The child is allowed to save the credits he earns for desirable behavior and later swap them for desirable objects or privileges. In other words, he gets tokens and spends them on things like going to the movies, playing outside, watching TV, or, if his parents allow it, even money. In any case, the exchange rate should be determined ahead of time.

Chapter 10
Step 3: Structured Routines

A structured routine is a schedule of daily activities and chores that has been meticulously prepared and adhered to. It gives a regular and orderly framework for those with ADHD to follow throughout the day. People with ADHD frequently struggle with concentration, impulsivity, and time management, making it difficult to stay on track. They can better manage their time, reduce distractions, and increase their focus by following a scheduled regimen.

Setting particular hours for various tasks such as waking up, eating meals, working, studying, taking breaks, indulging in leisure activities, and going to bed is part of the scheduled routine. Having a set timetable for these tasks eliminates the need for those with ADHD to continually select what to do next, which can be daunting. Instead, they can just stick to the schedule and know what to expect throughout the day.

Calendars and to-do lists are common visual aids used to make the routine more accessible and clearer. Individuals with ADHD can use these graphic representations to visualize their schedules and keep track of their assignments and appointments. Visual cues are especially useful because they can enhance memory and serve as reminders, which is especially important for someone with ADHD who may struggle with forgetting.

A structured routine involves planned intervals between work and smooth transitions from one activity to the next, in addition to defined activity periods. Breaks are essential for recharging and avoiding burnout, and well-managed transitions can help people with ADHD adjust their focus more successfully without feeling bewildered or scattered.

A scheduled routine also highlights the need to stick to a constant sleep schedule. Adequate sleep is critical for ADHD patients because it affects their attention, focus, and emotional regulation. Individuals with ADHD can improve their general well-being and ability to control symptoms by going to bed and waking up at the same time every day.

STRUCTURED ROUTINES TO HELP MANAGE ADHD

MORNING ROUTINE

Wake up at the same time every day

Consistency is key in managing ADHD symptoms. Set an alarm for the same time each morning to establish a regular wake-up routine. Aim for a sufficient amount of sleep, ideally between 7-9 hours per night, to ensure you start the day feeling rested and refreshed.

Have a nutritious breakfast

Start your day with a balanced and nutritious breakfast. Include protein, complex carbohydrates, and healthy fats to provide sustained energy and support cognitive function. Avoid excessive sugar, as it can lead to energy spikes and crashes, affecting focus and attention.

Morning checklist or visual aid

Use a morning checklist or a visual aid like a calendar to guide you through your morning tasks. This can include brushing your teeth, washing your face, getting dressed, and other morning routines. Check off each task as you complete it, which can provide a sense of accomplishment and help you stay on track.

Allocate time for meditation or mindfulness

Consider incorporating a few minutes of meditation or mindfulness exercises in your morning routine. This practice can help you start the day with a clear and focused mind, reducing anxiety and enhancing overall well-being.

Set up your workspace

If you have work or study tasks to do in the morning, set up a clean and organized workspace. Minimize distractions by keeping the area tidy and removing unnecessary items from your immediate view.

Use timers for focused work

During work or study time, use timers or alarms to break your tasks into manageable chunks. Work on a specific task for a set amount of time (e.g., 25 minutes), and then take a short break (e.g., 5 minutes). This technique, known as the Pomodoro technique, can help maintain focus and prevent burnout.

Consider using noise-canceling headphones or background music

Depending on your preferences, you might find that noise-canceling headphones or background music help you concentrate better. Experiment with different options to see what works best for you.

Take regular breaks

Between work or study blocks, remember to take short breaks to recharge. During these breaks, engage in physical activities, such as stretching or a quick walk, to increase alertness and maintain productivity.

Use a to-do list or task manager

Keep track of your ongoing and upcoming tasks using a to-do list or task manager. This can help you prioritize your activities, ensuring you focus on what needs to be done first.

Set priorities for the afternoon

Before moving into the afternoon, identify the most critical tasks you need to accomplish. This way, you can approach the afternoon with a clear plan and avoid feeling overwhelmed.

By following this structured morning routine, individuals with ADHD can establish a solid foundation for the rest of their day. It sets the tone for better time management, increased focus, and reduced stress. Remember that creating a routine that suits your individual needs and preferences is essential for its effectiveness. Don't hesitate to make adjustments and tailor the routine to work best for you.

WORK/SCHOOL TIME

The Work/School Time portion of the structured routine focuses on establishing a productive and focused work or study environment. It helps individuals with ADHD manage their tasks, maintain concentration, and avoid feeling overwhelmed.

Follow this practical guide for this part of the routine:

Designate Specific Blocks of Time

Divide your work or school tasks into focused blocks of time. For instance, you can dedicate 25-30 minutes to a specific task, followed by a short break. This technique, known as the Pomodoro technique, can help maintain focus and prevent feeling overwhelmed.

Here's a more practical illustration:

Let's say you have a study session ahead of you, and you need to review for an upcoming exam. Instead of trying to study for an extended period without breaks, you can break down your study time into specific blocks using the Pomodoro technique:

1. **Set a Timer:** Begin by setting a timer for a specific interval, such as 25 minutes. This time interval is often referred to as a "Pomodoro." It's named after the tomato-shaped kitchen timer used by the creator of this technique.
2. **Study Intensely:** During the 25-minute Pomodoro, focus solely on studying the material you need to review for the exam. Avoid distractions like checking your phone or browsing the internet. If any distractions arise, acknowledge them and return your focus to your study material.

3. **Take a Short Break:** When the timer goes off after 25 minutes, take a short break of around 5 minutes. Use this time to stretch, walk around, or do something enjoyable but unrelated to your studies.

4. **Start the Next Pomodoro:** After the 5-minute break, set the timer for another 25-minute study session (Pomodoro). Once again, concentrate on your study material and try to avoid distractions.

5. **Longer Break After 4 Pomodoros:** After completing four Pomodoros (25-minute study sessions) and taking short breaks between each one, take a longer break of around 15-30 minutes. Use this break to refresh your mind and recharge.

6. **Repeat the Cycle:** Continue this cycle of focused study sessions (Pomodoros) followed by short breaks, with a longer break every four Pomodoros. Repeat the cycle until you've completed the amount of study time you've allocated for the day.

The Pomodoro technique helps you break your study time into manageable chunks, making it easier to maintain focus and productivity. The specific time intervals can be adjusted based on individual preferences and attention span. Some people may find 25 minutes too short or too long, so feel free to experiment and find what works best for you.

Set Up a Clean and Organized Workspace

Ensure your workspace is clean, clutter-free, and organized. Remove any unnecessary items that might distract you during work or study sessions. Have all the essential materials and tools within reach to avoid interruptions.

Use Alarms or Timers

Set alarms or timers to signal the start and end of each work or study block. This creates a sense of structure and helps you transition smoothly from one task to another.

Prioritize Tasks

Before starting your work or study session, identify the most important tasks that need to be completed. Tackle these tasks first to avoid feeling overwhelmed by multiple responsibilities.

Here's a more practical illustration of how to do this:

Let's say you have a list of tasks to complete for the day, including work assignments, household chores, and personal errands:

1. Create a Task List: Start by writing down all the tasks you need to accomplish for the day. Include both big and small tasks. For example:

- Complete a work report.
- Respond to urgent work emails.
- Do the laundry.
- Buy groceries.
- Prepare dinner.
- Call the doctor to schedule an appointment.

2. Identify Urgent and Important Tasks: Go through your task list and identify tasks that are both urgent and important. These are the tasks that have deadlines or time-sensitive requirements and also have a significant impact on your day or life. For example:

- Completing the work report is urgent because it's due by the end of the day, and it's essential for your job.
- Responding to urgent work emails is also time-sensitive and critical for work-related communication.

3. Prioritize High-Impact Tasks: Next, look for tasks that may not be urgent but have a high impact on your goals or well-being. These tasks can significantly contribute to your overall productivity and happiness. For example:

- Buying groceries is not urgent, but it's crucial for having food for the week and maintaining a healthy diet.
- Doing the laundry is not time-sensitive, but having clean clothes can make your day more comfortable and organized.

4. Consider Time and Effort Required: Take into account the time and effort required for each task. Some tasks may be quick and straightforward, while others may be more time-consuming or require more mental focus. For example:

- Preparing dinner may take some time, but it's essential for your well-being and can be done later in the day when you have more energy.
- Scheduling a doctor's appointment may only take a few minutes, so you can do it quickly.

5. Order Tasks by Priority: After considering urgency, importance, time, and effort, order your tasks by priority. Start with the most urgent and important tasks first, followed by high-impact tasks, and then other tasks that can be completed later in the day.

6. Focus on One Task at a Time: As you begin your day, focus on one task at a time. Avoid trying to multitask, as it can reduce productivity and increase the risk of mistakes.

7. Review and Adjust Throughout the Day: As you complete tasks, review your list and adjust priorities if needed. New tasks or changes in circumstances may arise, so be flexible and adapt accordingly.

By prioritizing tasks, you can approach your day with a clear plan, maintain focus on critical responsibilities, and reduce the risk of feeling overwhelmed. Prioritization allows you to make the most of your time and energy, ensuring that you accomplish the most important tasks efficiently.

Minimize Distractions

Minimize potential distractions during work or study time. Consider using noise-canceling headphones or background music to create a focused environment, especially if you work or study in a busy or noisy area.

Stay Hydrated and Take Short Breaks

Keep a water bottle nearby, and remember to stay hydrated throughout your work or study session. Take short breaks, about 5 minutes, after each focused block to recharge and avoid mental fatigue.

Stay on Task

During each work or study block, try to stay on task and avoid multitasking, as it can be counterproductive for individuals with ADHD. Focus on one task at a time to maintain productivity.

Review Progress

At the end of each work or study block, take a moment to review what you've accomplished. Celebrate your achievements, even if they are small, as positive reinforcement can help boost motivation.

REMEMBER: Be kind to yourself. If you encounter challenges or encounter distractions during your work or study time, be kind to yourself. Recognize that ADHD can present unique difficulties and focus on progress rather than perfection.

LUNCH

Lunch is an essential part of the structured routine for individuals with ADHD, as it provides an opportunity to refuel and maintain focus for the rest of the day. Here's a practical approach to incorporating lunch into the routine:

Set a Consistent Lunchtime

Schedule a specific time each day for lunch. For example, aim to have lunch at 12:30 PM. Consistency helps regulate your body's internal clock, and having a designated lunchtime ensures you take a much-needed break during the busy day.

Plan Your Lunch Options

Consider planning your lunch options ahead of time. This can involve meal prepping or creating a list of healthy lunch ideas that you enjoy. Having a variety of options makes it easier to choose a balanced and nutritious meal each day.

Incorporate Protein, Healthy Fats, and Vegetables

Aim for a well-balanced meal that includes a good source of protein (e.g., lean meat, fish, tofu, or legumes), healthy fats (e.g., avocado, nuts, or olive oil), and plenty of vegetables. The combination of nutrients provides sustained energy and supports cognitive function.

Quick and Easy Preparation

Choose lunch options that are quick and easy to prepare, especially if you have limited time during your lunch break. Simple meals like salads with pre-cooked chicken, quinoa bowls, or whole-grain sandwiches can be both nutritious and time-efficient.

Pack Your Lunch (if applicable)

If you're going to school or work, consider packing your lunch the night before or in the morning. Having your lunch ready to go saves time and ensures you have a healthy option available.

Avoid Heavy or Sugary Foods

Heavy, greasy, or sugary foods may lead to energy crashes and reduced focus in the afternoon. Opt for light and nutritious meals that provide sustained energy without the post-lunch slump.

Mindful Eating

During lunchtime, practice mindful eating. Take your time to chew your food thoroughly, savor the flavors, and enjoy the meal. Eating mindfully can enhance digestion and help you feel more satisfied with your food.

Stay Hydrated

Alongside your lunch, don't forget to drink water to stay hydrated. Proper hydration is essential for cognitive function and overall well-being.

Take a Break

Utilize your lunch break as an opportunity to step away from work or study tasks. Taking a mental break can help recharge your focus for the rest of the day.

REMEMBER: By following this structured approach to lunch, individuals with ADHD can ensure they have a balanced and nourishing meal that supports their cognitive function and overall well-being. Planning ahead and making mindful choices can contribute to a positive and productive afternoon, keeping you energized and focused throughout the rest of your day. Remember to tailor your lunchtime routine to suit your preferences and dietary needs for the best results.

AFTERNOON

If you want to keep your productivity and concentration levels high throughout the day, the afternoon routine is a must. Managing your time well entails keeping up with your work or studies, remaining organized with a to-do list or task organizer, and prioritizing what you have to do.

Continue Focused Work/Study Blocks

After lunch, continue with your work or study tasks using the focused blocks technique. Set a timer for a specific interval, like 25 minutes, and concentrate on one task during that time. Take short breaks of about 5 minutes between each focused block to recharge.

Use a To-Do List or Task Manager

Keep track of your ongoing and upcoming tasks using a to-do list or task manager. Write down the tasks you need to complete for the afternoon, including any new ones that may have come up during the day.

Prioritize Tasks

Review your to-do list and identify the most important tasks for the afternoon. Consider their urgency and impact on your goals. Prioritize these tasks to avoid feeling overwhelmed, and ensure you address essential responsibilities first.

Break Down Larger Tasks

If you have larger or more complex tasks on your list, break them down into smaller, more manageable subtasks. This makes them less intimidating and helps you approach them step by step.

Let's consider this practical illustration:

Let's say you have a research paper to complete for your school or work. Writing a research paper can be a daunting task, so breaking it down into smaller subtasks can make the process more manageable:

1. **Select a Topic:** Choose a topic for your research paper. Ensure it aligns with your assignment guidelines and interests you.

2. **Conduct Research:** Begin by conducting research on your chosen topic. Collect relevant sources, such as articles, books, or academic papers.

3. **Create an Outline:** Develop an outline for your research paper. Organize your main points and supporting evidence into logical sections.

4. **Write the Introduction:** Start by writing the introduction of your research paper. Introduce the topic, provide background information, and state your thesis statement.

5. **Write Body Paragraphs:** Focus on writing one body paragraph at a time. Each paragraph should address a specific point from your outline and include supporting evidence.

6. **Cite Sources:** As you write, remember to cite your sources properly using the appropriate citation style (e.g., APA, MLA).

7. **Write the Conclusion:** Craft a conclusion that summarizes your main points and restates your thesis in a conclusive manner.

8. **Edit and Revise:** After completing the first draft, take time to edit and revise your research paper. Check for coherence, clarity, and grammar errors.

9. **Seek Feedback:** If possible, seek feedback from peers, teachers, or colleagues. Incorporate constructive feedback to improve your paper.

10. **Finalize and Submit:** Make final adjustments based on the feedback received and ensure your paper meets all requirements. Submit the completed research paper by the deadline.

Breaking down the research paper into these smaller subtasks allows you to focus on one aspect of the project at a time. Completing each subtask provides a sense of accomplishment and motivates you to move on to the next step. This approach helps you manage your time more effectively and reduces the stress associated with tackling a large project all at once.

Review Progress

After completing each focused block or task, take a moment to review your progress. Acknowledge what you've accomplished, and use this positive reinforcement to stay motivated.

Adjust Priorities if Needed

As the afternoon progresses, be flexible with your priorities. New tasks or urgent requests may come up, so adjust your to-do list accordingly and focus on what's most important at the moment.

Take Short Mental Breaks

In addition to the short breaks between focused blocks, consider taking a short mental break during the afternoon. Step away from your work or study area for a few minutes to refresh your mind and prevent mental fatigue.

Stay Hydrated

Remember to drink water throughout the afternoon to stay hydrated. Dehydration can affect cognitive function and focus, so keep a water bottle nearby and take sips regularly.

Celebrate Achievements

As you complete tasks and reach milestones in your afternoon routine, take a moment to celebrate your achievements. Recognizing your progress can boost your confidence and motivation.

EVENING

The evening section of the structured routine focuses on winding down from the day's activities and preparing for a restful night's sleep. Following this routine can help individuals with ADHD establish healthy sleep habits and improve overall well-being.

To effectively carry out the evening routine, follow the guide below:

Plan a Designated Dinner Time

Set a specific time for dinner each evening to establish a consistent mealtime routine. Aim for a relaxed and enjoyable dinner, and try to avoid eating too close to bedtime to allow for proper digestion.

Limit Screen Time Before Bedtime

As the evening progresses, start to limit screen time from electronic devices like phones, computers, and televisions. The blue light emitted by screens can interfere with your body's production of melatonin, a hormone that helps regulate sleep.

Engage in Calming Activities

Wind down with calming activities to signal to your body that it's time to relax and prepare for sleep. Consider reading a book, writing in a journal to reflect on the day, or taking a warm bath.

Set a Consistent Bedtime

Determine a consistent bedtime that allows for enough restful sleep. Aim for around 7-9 hours of sleep per night, as adequate sleep is essential for managing ADHD symptoms and maintaining overall well-being.

Tip: Here's an example of how the evening routine could be structured:

1. **6:30 PM:** Plan and prepare dinner. Avoid heavy or spicy foods close to bedtime.
2. **7:00 PM:** Sit down for a relaxed dinner with family or friends. Enjoy the meal and engage in pleasant conversation.
3. **8:00 PM:** Start winding down from the day's activities. Dim the lights to create a calming atmosphere.
4. **8:30 PM:** Limit screen time. Put away electronic devices and engage in screen-free activities like reading or listening to soft music.
5. **9:00 PM:** Take a warm bath or engage in other relaxing activities to unwind.
6. **9:30 PM:** Write in a journal to reflect on the day or practice mindfulness exercises.
7. **10:00 PM:** Set a consistent bedtime and start preparing for sleep. Create a calming bedtime routine, such as stretching or deep breathing exercises.
8. **10:30 PM:** Go to bed and aim to get 7-9 hours of restful sleep.

By following this structured evening routine, individuals with ADHD can create a peaceful and consistent bedtime routine, improving their sleep quality and overall well-being. Remember to adapt the routine to fit your personal preferences and schedule, and be consistent in maintaining healthy sleep habits for the best results.

GENERAL TIPS

General tips are essential for the success of any structured routine, including one designed to help individuals with ADHD. These tips provide additional support and encouragement, making it easier to maintain the routine and achieve positive outcomes.

Keep the Routine Posted in a Visible Place

Print or write down the structured routine and place it in a visible location, such as on a bulletin board, the refrigerator, or your bedroom wall. Having the routine displayed prominently serves as a constant reminder of the tasks and activities you need to follow throughout the day.

For individuals with ADHD, visual cues and reminders play a crucial role in managing time and staying organized. Having the routine displayed in a prominent location serves as a constant visual reminder of the tasks and activities they need to complete throughout the day. It helps maintain focus, reduces forgetfulness, and promotes a sense of structure and predictability.

Select a visible location that aligns with your daily routine and lifestyle. Common places to post the routine include:

1. **Refrigerator:** Attach the routine to the refrigerator door with magnets. The kitchen is a central area that you're likely to visit multiple times a day, making it an ideal spot for a visual reminder.
2. **Bedroom Wall:** Place the routine near your bed or on the bedroom wall. It will be one of the first things you

see when you wake up and can serve as a guide for starting your morning routine.

3. **Bulletin Board:** If you have a bulletin board or a designated organization area in your home, pin the routine there. This location can centralize important information and schedules.

Make the routine visually appealing and easy to read. You can use different colors for each section of the routine or add symbols or icons to represent specific activities. A clear and concise format will ensure that the information is quickly accessible.

As your routine evolves or changes, update the displayed routine accordingly. Use removable adhesive materials or laminated sheets so that you can easily modify or replace sections of the routine when needed.

Also, if you share a living space with family members or room-mates, inform them about the purpose of the routine and request their support. Encourage them to remind you gently if they notice you deviating from the routine or to celebrate your accomplishments when you stick to them consistently.

BE FLEXIBLE AND WILLING TO ADJUST

Flexibility is key when implementing a structured routine for individuals with ADHD. Life can be unpredictable, and unexpected events or changes in plans may arise. Being willing to adjust the routine allows for adaptability and ensures that the routine remains a helpful tool rather than a source of stress.

There is no doubt that life is full of uncertainties, and rigid adherence to a fixed routine may not always be feasible. By being flexible, individuals with ADHD can navigate unexpected events, disruptions, or changes in their daily schedule without feeling overwhelmed or defeated. Flexibility allows them to maintain a structured approach while acknowledging the realities of life's twists and turns.

Here's how to incorporate flexibility:

1. **Accept Real-Life Situations:** Embrace the understanding that real-life situations are sometimes beyond your control. Whether it's a last-minute meeting at work, a sudden family event, or unexpected weather conditions, acknowledge that adjustments to the routine may be necessary.
2. **Build in Buffer Time:** When creating the routine, consider adding buffer time between tasks or activities. Buffer time provides some breathing space to handle unexpected events without significantly disrupting the entire schedule.
3. **Prioritize and Reorganize:** In the face of unforeseen events, prioritize essential tasks and adjust the routine accordingly. Determine which tasks can be postponed and which ones require immediate attention. Reorganize the routine to accommodate the most critical responsibilities.
4. **Practice Mindfulness and Stress Management:** If unexpected changes occur, practice mindfulness techniques to stay centered and manage stress. Taking a moment to breathe and assess the situation can help you approach adjustments to the routine with a clear mind.
5. **Reflect and Learn:** After a day with adjustments to the routine, take time to reflect on how you managed the changes and any challenges you encountered. Use these experiences as learning opportunities to refine the routine and make it more resilient to future changes.

A practical example of flexibility:

Let's say you have a structured routine that includes a morning exercise routine. However, one morning, you wake up feeling unwell and unable to exercise. Instead of feeling defeated, you practice flexibility:

- **Be Kind to Yourself:** Recognize that taking care of your health is a priority. Listen to your body and acknowledge that it's okay to skip the exercise routine for today.
- **Adjust the Routine:** Reorganize your morning to allow for extra rest and recovery. Focus on essential morning tasks and allocate additional time for self-care.
- **Consider the Afternoon:** If you feel better later in the day, you can consider doing a light exercise routine in the afternoon if it fits your schedule and energy level.

Chapter 11
Step 4: Time Management Strategies

People with ADHD frequently struggle with time management. They are prone to losing track of time, procrastinating, and underestimating the amount of time required to finish their activities. Or maybe they're doing things in the wrong order.

Many individuals with ADHD frequently fall into the trap of focusing so intensely on a single job that nothing else gets done, a condition described as "hyper-focusing." These kinds of issues can leave you feeling dissatisfied and impatient with yourself. However, there are techniques you can learn to maximize your time and increase your work productivity tenfold.

TIME MANAGEMENT TIPS

The passage of time can appear extremely different to an adult with ADHD than it does to other people. For example, if you are assigned a large, redundant assignment, the passage of time may appear to be exceedingly slow. On the other side, when you're doing something you enjoy, time seems to fly by. Wearing a watch is the oldest method in the book for calibrating oneself with other people.

Turn Into a Clock-Watcher

Wear a wristwatch all the time, or keep a prominent wall clock or desk clock to see how much time has gone since you began working on a task. Take note of the time when you begin a task. You might even want to physically write down the time so you don't forget when you started.

Use Countdown Timers

Give yourself a time limit for each work, and then set an alarm to play music or sound when the timer runs out. Set up many alarms to go off at regular intervals if you're working on a larger assignment so you're continually alerted and reminded to work on it.

Give Yourself More Time for Tasks

If you're like most other adults with ADHD, you're terrible at calculating timetables; it's difficult to even estimate how much time you'll need to finish something. You'll need to come up with a big number so that you have more than enough time for everything. For example, if you believe it will only take you thirty minutes to go grocery shopping, add ten to twenty minutes to your estimate, and you'll be OK.

Plan To Arrive Early and Constantly Remind Yourself of Your Plan

When scheduling appointments, pretend that they are at least fifteen minutes earlier than the actual time you need to meet. Set additional reminders to get ready and leave the house on time. This will save you from frantically racing around the house and squandering valuable time because you can't find your keys or phone.

TIPS FOR PRIORITIZING TASKS FOR EFFECTIVE TIME MANAGEMENT

Adults with ADHD frequently struggle with impulse control and tend to leap from one task to the next. Most of the time, both activities are completely unrelated, and neither task is ever accomplished. People with ADHD find it difficult to complete or even attempt to complete major projects.

Here are a few tips to help you break this terrible habit and better manage your time:

Decide On What to Do First

Consider which task on your list is the most important, second most important, and so on.

Take Each Step One At a Time

Break down larger jobs into smaller, more manageable steps. For example, if the large task is to "peel and slice a pineapple," you can break it down into individual steps such as "cut off the top with the leaves," "chop off the bottom," "allow the pineapple to stand, and then take off the hard outer skin of the pineapple," and so on. This may appear to be a ridiculous example, but the same technique can be used for nearly any activity you need to finish, especially if it appears to be vast and scary at first.

Maintain Focus on the Task

Avoid being sidetracked by simply working on the activities on your schedule and perhaps even using a timer to help you focus on finishing that task. Remove all distractions from the room and, if necessary, set up a distinct workspace where you will complete any vital activities.

Understand When It's Okay to Say No

If you are especially affected by ADHD's impulsive symptoms, you may have difficulty agreeing to work on too many tasks or saying yes to too many social gatherings. It doesn't matter if you can stuff everything into your plan; the problem is that just glancing at a packed schedule might make you feel extremely overwhelmed. And if you don't give yourself enough time to work on projects, the quality of your work suffers.

When someone asks you to do something for them, first examine your schedule and say no if there is just no room in it. Using a calendar app on your smartphone to keep track of your schedule is a terrific way to stay organized. Create one and make it a practice to review it before agreeing to anything, no matter how minor!

Chapter 12
Step 5: Organization Skills

People with ADHD have an inability to focus and are easily distracted, making organizing one of the most difficult issues that individuals with ADHD confront. If you have recently been diagnosed with ADHD, simply looking at all the clutter and mess in your home may make you feel overwhelmed, primarily because you do not know where to begin.

Learning to divide major jobs into smaller "sub-tasks" and developing and adhering to a simple organizational system will make things easier. Keeping organized requires the usage of several routines and frameworks. Use all of the tools at your disposal, including daily planners and setting reminders. By applying these organizing tactics, you will be well on your way to having an orderly and clutter-free house.

STRATEGY 1: DEVELOP STRUCTURE AND NEATNESS HABITS, AND KEEP ON DOING THEM

To begin organizing a room, sort the debris into several groups. Essentially, you will be determining which items you still require, which you can store, and which you can discard. Make a habit of writing lists and carrying a tiny notebook with you so you may take notes whenever you need to. You must retain your new habits and structures by incorporating them into your regular routines; in other words, make them a part of your daily life until they become second nature to you.

Create/Set Aside Space for Storage

You must first determine what items you require on a daily basis and then make room for them in your home. Place a bowl on your nightstand or a side table at the front entrance, for example, to hold your keys, wallet, spare change, and other items that you need but frequently misplace. Place a small waste bin nearby so you may discard any items in your pockets that you no longer use, such as ticket stubs, receipts, wrappers, and other odd items.

Make Use of a Calendar App or a Daily Planner

Whether you want cutting-edge technology or prefer to keep things old-school, there are tools available to help you stay organized. You may use your smartphone or computer's calendar app to help you remember key events and appointments; you can even set alarms to remind you days in advance to ensure that you don't forget. You can also acquire a smartwatch that syncs with your smartphone so that you don't even have to open your phone; the reminders will be sent directly to your wrist.

Learn To Create and Use Lists and Notes

Lists and notes can help you keep track of your usual tasks, ongoing projects, forthcoming deadlines, and any appointments you have that day. If you decide to utilize an old-school day planner, keep your lists inside to avoid losing them. You can utilize "to-do" apps on your smartphone if you choose that path.

Deal With the Clutter Right Now

Dealing with clutter right away is one of the easiest strategies to avoid forgetting and procrastination. File papers as soon as you see them, tidy up minor mistakes as soon as you notice them and return phone calls and messages as soon as you are reminded of them. If a work can be completed in less than two minutes, do it straight away rather than later. This is a habit you can cultivate, and you will find yourself procrastinating less over time.

STRATEGY 2: REGAIN CONTROL OF YOUR PAPER TRAIL

When you have ADHD, dealing with paperwork can be a major challenge, and this may contribute to your disorganization. But what if I told you that you can get rid of the apparently unending stacks of paper on your kitchen counter, nightstand, or workplace desk? All you need to do is set aside some time to devise a strategy for organizing documents that work for you.

Sort Your Mail Daily

You will only need a few minutes to sift through the varied mail that you receive on a daily basis, and you can begin immediately after taking it out of the mailbox or at a set time each day. It will be quite beneficial if you have a separate area for mail, preferably one with several compartments: one for filing, one for quick action, and one for those that should go straight to the trash.

Go Paperless

Nowadays, you may simply request that your billers send you an electronic copy of your bills via email. In this manner, you're essentially killing two birds with one stone: you're getting rid of much of the paper clutter you have to deal with while also helping the environment.

Start a Filing System

Use file dividers or separate folders for crucial documents such as medical records, receipts, income statements, and coupons. Label and color-code each folder so that the next time you need to find something, you can do it much faster.

Chapter 13
Step 6: Exercise And Physical Activity

In the realm of managing ADHD (Attention Deficit Hyperactivity Disorder), the importance of exercise and physical activity shines as a beacon of hope. For individuals navigating the challenges of ADHD, regular exercise offers a transformative pathway to enhanced focus, reduced impulsivity, and improved well-being.

This dynamic duo of physical movement and mental engagement opens the door to a world of benefits, empowering individuals to thrive amidst the intricacies of ADHD. In this chapter, we will explore the myriad advantages of exercise, discovering how it can be harnessed as a powerful tool for managing ADHD and fostering a balanced, fulfilling life. We will also look at the various exercises to embark on for improved attention, mood, and overall quality of life for those with ADHD.

BENEFITS OF EXERCISE AND PHYSICAL ACTIVITIES IN DEALING WITH ADHD

Improved Focus and Attention

Regular exercise has been shown to increase the production of neurotransmitters like dopamine and norepinephrine, which are essential for attention and focus. As a result, individuals with ADHD experience improved concentration, allowing them to stay more engaged and attentive during tasks.

Reduced Hyperactivity and Impulsivity

Physical activity provides a constructive outlet for excess energy often associated with ADHD. Engaging in exercise helps channel hyperactivity in a productive manner and reduces impulsive behaviors.

Enhanced Executive Functioning

Exercise has a positive impact on executive functions, including planning, organization, and time management. These cognitive skills are often challenging for individuals with ADHD, and regular physical activity can help sharpen them.

Mood Elevation and Stress Reduction

Exercise triggers the release of endorphins, which are natural mood enhancers. It helps alleviate stress, anxiety, and feelings of restlessness commonly experienced by those with ADHD.

Better Sleep Quality

Consistent physical activity contributes to improved sleep quality. Adequate sleep is crucial for managing ADHD symptoms and supporting overall well-being.

Increased Self-Esteem and Confidence

Engaging in regular physical activities can lead to a sense of achievement and increased self-esteem. Accomplishing exercise goals boosts confidence and encourages a positive self-image.

Healthy Coping Mechanism

Exercise provides a healthy coping mechanism for managing stress and emotional challenges. It serves as an outlet for releasing pent-up emotions and promoting emotional regulation.

Brain Health and Cognitive Enhancement

Exercise has neuroprotective effects, promoting brain health and cognitive function. It fosters better neural connectivity and may even enhance learning abilities for individuals with ADHD.

Social Interaction and Community Building

Participating in group exercises or sports facilitates social interaction and community building. Social connections can help combat feelings of isolation and loneliness.

Sustainable Lifestyle Habits

Adopting regular exercise and physical activity as part of a daily routine encourages the development of sustainable healthy lifestyle habits. This holistic approach positively impacts overall physical and mental health.

VARIOUS EXERCISES AND PHYSICAL ACTIVITIES TO HELP MANAGE ADHD

1. AEROBIC EXERCISES

Activities that get the heart rate up and increase blood flow to the brain are particularly beneficial.

Below are a few examples of aerobic exercises you can practice:

A. Running or Jogging

Running or jogging can be a highly effective form of exercise to achieve maximum results, especially when it comes to cardiovascular fitness, calorie burning, and overall well-being for people with ADHD.

Performance Tips:

- *Warm-Up Properly.* Before starting your run or jog, warm up your body with dynamic stretching or light aerobic exercises. Warming up helps prepare your muscles and cardiovascular system for the upcoming activity, reducing the risk of injury.
- *Start Slow and Gradually Increase Intensity.* If you're new to running or jogging, start at a comfortable pace and gradually increase your speed and intensity over time. This approach allows your body to adapt to the demands of the activity and reduces the risk of overexertion.

- *Focus on Proper Form.* Maintain good running form to prevent unnecessary strain on your body. Keep your head and chest up, shoulders relaxed, and arms bent at a 90-degree angle. Land mid-foot or forefoot with each stride and avoid overstriding.
- *Incorporate Interval Training.* Intervals involve alternating between periods of high-intensity running and periods of rest or low-intensity jogging. This technique can boost cardiovascular fitness and help burn more calories in a shorter amount of time.
- *Stay Hydrated.* Ensure you're adequately hydrated before, during, and after your run or jog. Dehydration can affect performance and recovery, so drink water or electrolyte beverages as needed.

B. Cycling

Cycling requires continuous attention to the road, traffic, and surroundings. This level of focus can help individuals with ADHD improve their ability to concentrate on a single task for an extended period, promoting better attention skills in other areas of life.

Cycling also provides an outlet for excess energy and restless-ness commonly experienced by individuals with ADHD. Engaging in this physical activity helps channel hyperactivity in a constructive way, reducing impulsive behaviors and promoting a sense of calm.

Like many forms of exercise, cycling triggers the release of dopamine and endorphins in the brain. These neurotransmitters play a crucial role in mood regulation and can help alleviate symptoms of anxiety and depression often associated with ADHD.

Performance Tips:

- **Safety First:** Always wear a properly fitted helmet and any other necessary safety gear. Follow traffic rules, signal your intentions, and be aware of your surroundings while cycling on roads.
- **Ensure to Start Gradually:** If you're new to cycling or haven't ridden in a while, start with shorter rides at a comfortable pace and gradually increase the distance and intensity.
- **Plan Scenic Routes:** Cycling allows you to explore new areas and enjoy nature. Plan scenic routes or bike paths to make your rides more enjoyable.
- **Hydration and Nutrition:** Bring water and snacks, especially for longer rides, to stay hydrated and maintain energy levels.
- **Proper Posture:** Maintain good posture while cycling, keeping your back straight and your hands relaxed on the handlebars.
- **Stretch After Riding:** After a cycling session, perform stretching exercises to help prevent muscle tightness and enhance flexibility.
- **Bike Maintenance:** Regularly inspect and maintain your bike to ensure it's safe and in good working condition.

C. Dancing

Dancing requires individuals to focus on movements, rhythm, and coordination. This focused attention during dancing can help improve concentration and increase attention span, which is often challenging for individuals with ADHD.

Dancing provides a constructive outlet for excess physical energy and restlessness commonly experienced by individuals with ADHD. Engaging in rhythmic movements can help release pent-up energy and reduce impulsivity.

Above all, dancing is fun and enjoyable! Engaging in an activity that brings joy can have a positive impact on mental health and overall life satisfaction.

2. SPORTS AND TEAM ACTIVITIES

Engaging in physical activities like sports not only provides physical exercise but also offers unique opportunities for social interaction, skill development, and emotional growth.

Participating in sports requires sustained attention and focus on the game or activity. Regularly engaging in sports can help individuals with ADHD improve their ability to concentrate and stay present at the moment.

Also, regular sports participation involves adhering to a training schedule and being punctual for practices and games. This routine can help individuals with ADHD develop a sense of discipline and time management.

Below are some kinds of sports and team activities you can practice:

A. Soccer

Soccer, also known as football in many countries, is a dynamic and team-oriented sport that offers numerous benefits for individuals with ADHD (Attention Deficit Hyperactivity Disorder).

Soccer involves constant movement, running, and coordination, making it an excellent form of aerobic exercise. Regular physical activity through soccer helps reduce hyperactivity, improve focus, and promote better overall physical health.

B. Basketball

Basketball is a team sport that relies on effective communication, cooperation, and teamwork. Being part of a basketball team provides individuals with ADHD with opportunities to develop and improve their social skills, build positive relationships, and work together toward shared goals.

In addition, the fact that basketball involves running, jumping, dribbling, and shooting helps to provide a comprehensive workout. Constant movement and physical activity are essential for hyperactivity reduction and maximum physical health.

C. Martial Arts

Training in martial arts places a strong emphasis on self-control, reliability, and adherence to set procedures. This organized setting can encourage greater time management and organization abilities in those with ADHD.

Another aspect of martial arts training is that it instills emotional regulation. Learning to manage emotions during practice and competition can transfer to better self-regulation in daily life.

Chapter 14
Step 7: Mindfulness And Meditation

Mindfulness, the discipline of being fully present and engaged in the present moment, and Meditation, the practice of building inner serenity and clarity, complement each other wonderfully to create a comprehensive strategy for ADHD management.

Individuals with ADHD can learn to notice their thoughts and feelings without judgment through mindfulness, developing increased self-awareness and comprehension of their attention patterns. Meditation provides a haven of silence and peace, helping persons with ADHD to teach their minds to refocus and minimize impulsiveness.

Mindfulness and meditation work together to form a powerful ally, guiding individuals with ADHD toward improved concentration, improved emotional regulation, and a greater sense of self-acceptance. This winning combination enables people to address problems with renewed vigor and embrace their unique abilities.

In this chapter, we will look at various mindfulness and meditation techniques for managing ADHD.

MINDFULNESS AND MEDITATION TECHNIQUES FOR ADHD

1. Focused Breathing

Focused breathing, also known as breath awareness or mindful breathing, is a fundamental mindfulness meditation technique. It involves bringing your attention to the natural rhythm of your breath to cultivate present-moment awareness and promote relaxation. This practice is particularly helpful for individuals with ADHD, as it can help calm the mind and improve concentration.

Follow the steps below to practice Focused Breathing:

Step 1: Find a Comfortable Position

Sit in a comfortable chair or cross-legged on the floor. Make sure your back is straight but not tense. You can also lie down if sitting is uncomfortable.

Step 2: Choose a Focus Point

You can focus your attention on the sensation of the breath at your nostrils, the rise and fall of your abdomen, or the expansion and contraction of your chest. Pick one that feels most natural to you.

Step 3: Begin Breathing

Take a few deep breaths to relax your body and settle into the present moment. Then allow your breath to return to its natural rhythm.

Step 4: Observe the Breath

Pay full attention to your chosen focus point as you breathe. Notice the coolness of the air as you inhale and the warmth as you exhale. Feel the gentle rise and fall of your abdomen or the expansion and contraction of your chest.

Step 5: Stay Present

As you practice, your mind may wander, and that's okay. When you notice your thoughts drifting away, gently and non-judgmentally bring your focus back to your breath.

Step 6: Be Patient

Don't get frustrated with yourself if your mind wanders frequently. It's normal for the mind to wander, especially in the beginning. The practice is about acknowledging distractions and redirecting your focus back to the breath.

Step 7: Set a Timer

You can start with just a few minutes and gradually increase the duration as you become more comfortable with the practice. Setting a timer ensures that you stay on track and prevents the distraction of checking the clock.

REMEMBER: Consistency is key to seeing the benefits of focused breathing. Try to incorporate this practice into your daily routine, even if it's just for a few minutes each day.

2. Body Scan

Body scan is a mindfulness meditation technique that involves systematically focusing on different parts of your body, bringing your awareness to each area and observing any sensations or tension present. It is an excellent practice for individuals with ADHD as it promotes body awareness, relaxation, and a sense of grounding.

Step 1: Find a Quiet Space

Choose a comfortable and quiet place where you won't be disturbed during the practice. You can either sit in a comfortable chair or lie down on your back.

Step 2: Get Comfortable

If you're lying down, place a yoga mat or a soft surface beneath you. Make sure your body is in a relaxed position, arms at your sides and palms facing up. If sitting, ensure your back is straight but not tense and your hands can rest comfortably on your thighs.

Step 3: Begin with Breathing

Take a few deep breaths to relax your body and bring your focus to the present moment. Feel the sensations of the breath as you inhale and exhale.

Step 4: Start the Body Scan

Slowly begin to direct your attention to different parts of your body, starting from the top of your head and moving downward. You can use the following sequence or adjust it according to your preference:

- **Head:** Notice any sensations in your scalp, forehead, eyes, cheeks, and jaw. Release any tension you might be holding in these areas.
- **Neck and Shoulders:** Observe any tightness or discomfort in your neck and shoulders. Let go of any tension as you breathe.
- **Arms and Hands:** Shift your awareness to your upper arms, forearms, and hands. Be mindful of any sensations, warmth, or tingling in these areas.
- **Chest and Upper Back:** Pay attention to your chest and upper back as you breathe. Notice the rising and falling of your chest with each breath.
- **Abdomen:** Bring your awareness to your abdomen, feeling it expand with each inhale and contract with each exhale.
- **Lower Back and Hips:** Observe any sensations in your lower back and hips. Allow any tension to release with each breath.
- **Legs and Feet:** Finally, focus on your thighs, calves, and feet. Notice the contact of your feet with the ground if you're sitting or lying down.

Step 5: Explore Sensations

As you scan each body part, notice any sensations without judgment. If you encounter areas of tension or discomfort, try to breathe into those areas and visualize the tension melting away with each exhale.

Step 6: Stay Present

If your mind wanders during the body scan, gently redirect your focus back to the part of the body you were scanning.

Step 7: End with Full Body Awareness

After completing the body scan, take a few moments to bring your attention back to your entire body as a whole. Feel the sensation of your entire body resting or sitting peacefully.

NOTE: The body scan can be as short or as long as you'd like. It can range from a few minutes to half an hour or more. Start with a duration that feels comfortable and gradually extend it as you become more familiar with the practice.

3. Mindful Walking

Mindful walking, also known as walking meditation, is a form of mindfulness practice that involves walking slowly and deliberately while maintaining full awareness of each step and the surrounding environment. It can be a beneficial practice for individuals with ADHD as it provides a physical outlet for restless energy and helps improve focus and present-moment awareness.

Step 1: Find a Quiet Space

Choose a quiet and safe place to walk, preferably in nature or any area where you won't be disturbed or interrupted. It could be a park, garden, beach, or any serene location.

Step 2: Stand Still

Start by standing still for a moment, feeling the ground beneath your feet, and taking a few deep breaths to center yourself.

Step 3: Begin Walking Slowly

Start walking at a slow and comfortable pace. It's essential to walk slowly to give yourself enough time to be mindful of each step.

Step 4: Focus on Your Steps

Pay attention to the sensation of each step as you lift your foot, move it forward, and place it back down. Notice the shifting weight from one foot to the other.

Step 5: Observe Your Body

Be aware of how your body moves while walking. Notice the movement of your arms, the swaying of your hips, and the balance of your posture.

Step 6: Be Present

As you walk, bring your full attention to the act of walking. If your mind starts to wander, gently redirect your focus back to the physical sensations of walking.

Step 7: Engage Your Senses

Stay open to the sensory experience of walking. Notice the feeling of the ground beneath your feet, the sound of your foot-steps, the air against your skin, and any scents in the environment.

Step 8: Let Go of Distractions

If you encounter any distractions or thoughts, acknowledge them without judgment and then let them go, returning your attention to the walking process.

Step 9: Walking in a Circle

If you're in a limited space, you can walk in a circle or follow a designated path. The key is to maintain the same slow and mindful pace.

Step 10: Practice with Intention

You can set an intention for your mindful walking practice, such as cultivating gratitude, finding peace, or simply being present at the moment.

Step 11: End with Stillness

After walking mindfully for a period (e.g., 10-20 minutes), come to a stop. Stand still and take a moment to feel the effects of the practice. Notice how your body and mind feel after this mindful movement.

4. Guided Meditation

Guided meditation is a form of meditation where an instructor, either in person or through pre-recorded audio or video, leads you through the meditation process. This practice is especially helpful for individuals with ADHD, as the guidance and structure can help maintain focus and engagement throughout the meditation.

Below is a step-by-step guide to how guided meditation works:

Step 1: Choose a Guided Meditation

There are numerous guided meditation resources available online, including websites, apps, and videos. Look for guided meditations that are specifically designed for ADHD, stress reduction, focus, or relaxation.

Step 2: Find a Quiet Space

Select a quiet and comfortable place where you won't be disturbed during the meditation session. Sit or lie down in a relaxed posture.

Step 3: Play the Guided Meditation

Start the guided meditation recording or video of your choice. Close your eyes, take a few deep breaths to relax, and then follow the instructor's voice and guidance.

Step 4: Follow the Instructions

The instructor will likely lead you through various steps, such as focusing on your breath, relaxing your body, or visualizing peaceful scenes. Let yourself be fully present in each instruction.

Step 5: Stay Present

If your mind starts to wander, it's normal. The guided meditation instructor will often remind you to bring your focus back to the present moment, whether it's your breath, a specific visualization, or a body scan.

Step 6: Be Gentle with Yourself

If you find your mind wandering or if you get distracted, don't criticize yourself. Guided meditation is a practice, and it's natural for the mind to wander. Just gently bring your focus back to the guided instructions.

Step 7: Set a Timer

Some guided meditation sessions have a specific duration, while others may be open-ended. If there's no set duration, you can set a timer to ensure that you dedicate a specific amount of time to the practice.

Step 8: Experiment with Different Guides

Not all guided meditations will resonate with you in the same way. Explore different guides and instructors to find the ones that you connect with the most.

NOTE: To enjoy the full advantages of guided meditation, strive to incorporate it into your routine on a daily basis. Consistent practice can help you develop mindfulness abilities, increase your ability to focus and control ADHD symptoms.

5. Counting Meditation

Counting meditation is a simple and effective mindfulness technique that can help individuals with ADHD improve focus and concentration. It involves counting breaths and repetitions of a specific word or other objects as a way to anchor the mind and reduce distractions.

Step 1: Find a Quiet Space

Choose a quiet and comfortable place to sit or lie down. It's best to minimize distractions during the meditation practice.

Step 2: Start with Relaxation

Take a few deep breaths to relax your body and mind. Allow any tension or stress to release with each exhale.

Step 3: Choose a Focus

Decide on what you will count during the meditation. Common options include counting your breaths, counting repetitions of a specific word (e.g., "calm" or "peace"), or counting a set of objects (e.g., beads on a mala).

Step 4: Begin Counting

Start the meditation by focusing on your chosen object of counting. For example, if you're counting breaths, count each inhale and exhale cycle. If you're counting repetitions of a word, silently repeat the word with each breath.

Step 5: Maintain Focus

As you count, keep your attention on the counting process. If your mind wanders, gently bring your focus back to the counting without judgment.

Step 6: Count Up to a Set Number

You can choose to count up to a specific number (e.g., 10, 20, or 100) before starting again from one. This helps prevent your mind from wandering too far and adds structure to the practice.

Step 7: Be Patient and Gentle

Don't get frustrated if your mind wanders or if you lose count. It's normal for thoughts to arise. When you notice it, simply return your attention to the counting.

Step 8: Set a Timer

If you're not following a guided counting meditation, set a timer to determine the duration of your practice. Start with a few minutes and gradually increase the time as you become more comfortable.

Step 9: Conclude Mindfully

When the timer goes off or when you feel ready to end the meditation, take a few deep breaths and sit quietly for a moment to transition back to regular awareness.

6. Visualization

Visualization, also known as guided imagery or mental imagery, is a powerful mindfulness technique that involves creating vivid mental images or scenes in your mind's eye. It is especially beneficial for individuals with ADHD as it can help improve focus, reduce anxiety, and enhance relaxation.

Step 1: Find a Quiet Space

Choose a quiet and comfortable place where you can sit or lie down without distractions. Close your eyes to eliminate visual distractions from the external environment.

Relax Your Body: Take a few deep breaths to relax your body and release any tension. Let go of any thoughts or worries, and allow your mind to become more present.

Step 2: Choose a Visualization

Decide on the visualization you want to practice. It could be a serene natural setting, a favorite place from your past, or an imaginary scene that brings you peace and comfort.

Step 3: Engage Your Senses

Make the visualization as vivid as possible by engaging all your senses. Imagine the colors, shapes, sounds, smells, and textures of the scene you are visualizing.

Step 4: Step into the Scene

Mentally place yourself within the visualization. Imagine yourself fully present in the scene, as if you are there in person. Experience the environment around you and explore it with your mind.

Step 5: Stay Present

As you visualize, maintain your focus on the details of the scene. If your mind starts to wander, gently guide your attention back to the visualization.

Step 6: Add Movement or Action

To deepen the experience, you can add movement or actions to the visualization. For example, imagine yourself walking, sitting, or interacting with the elements in the scene.

Step 7: Stay Positive

Visualization can also be used for self-improvement and achieving goals. Imagine yourself succeeding, feeling confident, and achieving your aspirations.

Step 8: Practice Mindfully

Engage in visualization with an open and non-judgmental attitude. Allow the images to flow naturally, and let the experience unfold without forcing it.

Step 9: End with Gratitude

When you are ready to conclude the visualization, take a moment to express gratitude for the experience and the positive emotions it may have brought.

7. Five Senses Exercise

The Five Senses Exercise is a mindfulness practice that helps you become fully present by engaging your senses and grounding yourself in the current moment. It's a simple yet effective technique for individuals with ADHD to increase awareness and reduce distractions.

Step 1: Find a Quiet Space

Choose a quiet and comfortable place where you can sit or stand without interruptions.

Step 2: Take a Few Deep Breaths

Begin by taking a few deep breaths to relax and center yourself. Focus on the sensation of the breath as you inhale and exhale.

Step 3: Engage Your Senses

Start by becoming aware of each of your five senses one by one:

- **Sight:** Look around and notice five things you can see. Pay attention to the colors, shapes, and details of the objects.
- **Hearing:** Listen carefully and identify four things you can hear. It could be the sound of the wind, birds singing, or any other sounds in your environment.
- **Touch:** Notice three things you can touch or feel. It could be the texture of a surface, the sensation of your clothes against your skin, or the temperature of the air.
- **Smell:** Identify two things you can smell. Breathe deeply and notice any scents in the air, whether pleasant or neutral.
- **Taste:** Finally, focus on one thing you can taste. If you have something nearby to eat or drink, take a small bite or sip and savor the taste.

Step 4: Be Fully Present

As you engage each sense, be fully present and attentive to the experience. Try not to judge or analyze what you perceive, but simply notice it without attachment.

Step 5: Explore Your Environment

After completing the exercise, take a moment to appreciate your surroundings and the sensory richness of the present moment.

8. Labeling Thoughts

Labeling thoughts is a mindfulness method that entails recognizing and categorizing thoughts that come during meditation or daily activity. It is especially beneficial for those with ADHD since it helps generate space from distracting thoughts and promotes awareness of the thinking process.

Step 1: Set an Intention

Before starting the practice, set an intention to become more aware of your thoughts and how they influence your emotions and actions.

Step 2: Start Meditating

Find a quiet and comfortable place to sit for meditation. You can also practice this technique during everyday activities, not just formal meditation.

Step 3: Observe Your Thoughts

As you begin to meditate or go about your day, pay attention to the thoughts that arise in your mind. Notice the content of your thoughts without getting caught up in them.

Step 4: Label the Thoughts

When a thought comes up, mentally label it as "thinking" or use a simple word that describes the content of the thought. For example, if you're thinking about what to eat for lunch, label it as "planning" or "food."

Step 5: Be Objective

The goal is not to judge or analyze the thoughts but to observe them with a sense of objectivity. Avoid getting carried away by the thoughts and gently bring your focus back to the present moment.

Step 6: Non-Judgmental Approach

If you find yourself judging your thoughts or getting frustrated, acknowledge those feelings and bring your attention back to the labeling process without further judgment.

Step 7: Step Practice Regularly

Consistency is key to making this technique more effective. Set aside time each day to practice labeling thoughts during meditation or implement it throughout your daily routine.

Step 8: Extend Beyond Meditation

Once you get comfortable with the practice during meditation, you can apply it to your daily life. Whenever you notice distracting or unhelpful thoughts, label them as "thinking" and redirect your focus back to the task at hand.

Step 9: Combine with Breathing

You can also combine the labeling technique with focused breathing. As you label a thought, take a deep breath, and let it go as you return to the present moment.

9. Mindful Journaling

Mindful journaling is a type of self-reflection and mindfulness exercise that involves writing down your thoughts, feelings, and experiences while remaining conscious of the present moment. It is a helpful practice for people with ADHD because it stimulates self-expression, increases self-awareness, and aids in the management of emotions and stress.

Step 1: Set Aside Time

Choose a specific time during your day to dedicate to mindful journaling. It could be in the morning, before bed, or any other time that works best for you.

Step 2: Find a Quiet Space

Select a quiet and comfortable space where you can write without distractions. This could be a cozy corner in your home, a peaceful park, or any place where you feel at ease.

Step 3: Begin with Breath Awareness

Take a few deep breaths before you start journaling. Allow yourself to relax and center your focus on the present moment.

Step 4: Write Without Judgment

Start writing in your journal without judgment or self-censorship. Let the thoughts flow naturally, and don't worry about grammar or punctuation.

Step 5: Observe Your Thoughts and Feelings

As you write, be mindful of your thoughts and emotions. Acknowledge any feelings that arise without getting entangled in them.

Step 6: Describe Your Surroundings

If you're journaling in a specific location, take a moment to describe the environment around you. Notice the sights, sounds, smells, and sensations.

Step 7: Reflect on Your Experiences

Use your journal as a space to reflect on your experiences, challenges, and achievements. Consider how you responded to different situations and how you felt in those moments.

Step 8: Express Gratitude

Include gratitude in your journaling practice. Write down things you are grateful for, whether big or small, to foster a positive mindset.

Step 9: Practice Regularly

Make mindful journaling a regular habit. Even a few minutes of journaling each day can have a significant impact on your well-being and self-awareness.

Step 10: End with a Positive Note

Before closing your journal, write a positive affirmation or intention for the day or the next time you journal.

10. Loving-Kindness Meditation

Loving-Kindness Meditation, also known as Metta Meditation, is a mindfulness practice that involves cultivating feelings of love, compassion, and goodwill towards oneself and others. It is especially advantageous for people with ADHD since it can help them enhance their emotional well-being, reduce impulsivity, and develop positive relationships.

Step 1: Find a Comfortable Posture

Sit in a comfortable position with your back straight but not rigid. You can also lie down if sitting is uncomfortable.

Step 2: Begin with Breath Awareness

Take a few deep breaths to relax your body and mind. Allow yourself to settle into the present moment.

Step 3: Generate Loving Kindness Toward Yourself

Bring your attention to yourself and silently repeat phrases of loving-kindness, such as "May I be happy, May I be healthy, May I be safe, May I live with ease." Repeat each phrase several times, allowing the intention of loving-kindness to fill your heart.

Step 4: Extend Loving Kindness to Others

After focusing on yourself, extend the same feelings of love and compassion to others. You can start with someone close to you, like a family member or a friend. Repeat phrases like "May you be happy, May you be healthy, May you be safe, May you live with ease" while visualizing them in your mind.

Step 5: Expand to All Beings

Gradually broaden your focus to include more people and eventually all living beings. Repeat the phrases of loving-kindness for strangers, acquaintances, and even those you may find challenging.

Step 6: Stay Open and Non-Judgmental

As you practice, be open to whatever feelings arise. If you encounter resistance or difficulty in sending loving-kindness to certain individuals, approach it with compassion and non-judgment.

Step 7: Use Your Heart Center

Imagine the feelings of loving-kindness radiating from your heart center as you repeat the phrases. This visualization can help enhance the emotional aspect of the practice.

Step 8: Practice Regularly

Make Loving-Kindness Meditation a regular part of your mindfulness routine. You can practice it as a standalone meditation or integrate it into your daily mindfulness practice.

Step 9: End with Gratitude

When you're ready to conclude the meditation, take a moment to express gratitude for the experience and the positive intentions you've cultivated.

Chapter 15
Step 8: Limit Distractions

In previous chapters and steps, we talked about minimizing distractions. In this chapter, we are going to go into detail about what distractions mean for individuals with ADHD and how to limit distractions for effective results.

WHAT DOES DISTRACTION MEAN FOR ADHD INDIVIDUALS?

For individuals with ADHD (Attention Deficit Hyperactivity Disorder), distraction refers to the difficulty they experience in maintaining attention on a specific task or activity. It is a hall-mark symptom of the disorder and can manifest in various ways. Distractions can interfere with the person's ability to focus, concentrate, and complete tasks efficiently.

Let's look at some common aspects of distraction experienced by people with ADHD:

SOME COMMON ASPECTS OF DISTRACTIONS ADHD PEOPLE EXPERIENCE

1. Short Attention Span

Individuals with ADHD often have a limited attention span, making it challenging to sustain focus on tasks for extended periods. They may quickly become bored or lose interest in activities that require prolonged concentration.

2. Easily Distracted

Minor external stimuli, such as noises, movement, or visual cues, can divert the attention of individuals with ADHD from the task at hand. Even in relatively quiet environments, their minds may wander or jump to unrelated thoughts.

3. Difficulty Filtering

People with ADHD may struggle to filter out irrelevant information and prioritize what is essential for the task. This difficulty in filtering can lead to becoming overwhelmed by various stimuli and hinder efficient task completion.

4. Mind Wandering

ADHD individuals often experience frequent mind wandering, where their thoughts drift away from the current activity and shift to unrelated topics. This can lead to daydreaming or engaging in thoughts unrelated to the task.

5. Hyperfocus

Paradoxically, individuals with ADHD can also experience hyperfocus on tasks that genuinely interest or stimulate them. While this intense focus can be advantageous for activities they enjoy, it can make transitioning to less stimulating tasks even more challenging.

6. Impulsivity

Impulsivity is another common feature of ADHD. When a novel or exciting stimulus arises, individuals with ADHD may impulsively shift their attention to that stimulus, interrupting ongoing tasks or conversations.

7. Multitasking Difficulties

Contrary to common belief, multitasking can be challenging for individuals with ADHD. Attempting to focus on multiple tasks simultaneously can lead to decreased performance and increased errors.

8. Difficulty with Planning and Organization

Planning and organizing tasks can be difficult for individuals with ADHD. This can lead to a lack of structure, making it harder to stay on track and complete tasks systematically.

REMEMBER: Limiting distractions is a crucial strategy for managing ADHD (Attention Deficit Hyperactivity Disorder). As we know, ADHD is a neurodevelopmental disorder that affects a person's ability to focus, control impulses, and manage attention effectively. People with ADHD often struggle with maintaining attention on tasks or activities, leading to increased distractibility.

By minimizing distractions, individuals with ADHD can create a more conducive environment for concentration and task completion.

STEP-BY-STEP GUIDE TO LIMITING DISTRACTIONS

Step 1: Keep Electronics Away

Keep your phone or tablet out of sight if you know you'll be distracted by it. If you find yourself becoming obsessed with your devices, it may help to temporarily hide them or turn them off. Hide your electronic devices in a different room, a drawer, or some other inaccessible location.

Silence any distractions by turning off the radio or television. In addition, if you do any of your work on a computer or smartphone, you should look into installing some apps that help you stay focused and productive. Get a browser add-on that limits or completely prevents your access to social media, for instance.

Deactivate alerts. The distraction caused by your phone buzzing with an email or social media notification might last for up to 15 minutes. You can disable desktop notifications if they are too much of a distraction. The 'Do Not Disturb' function found on many modern smartphones will silence your phone's alerts while you're actively using it. Push alerts can be temporarily or permanently turned off as well.

Distractions can come from anything, such as flipping your phone over or leaving tabs open on your computer. Get rid of these interruptions if you want to win the battle.

Step 2: Use Website Blockers

This step is about using browser extensions or apps that can block access to distracting websites while you are working or studying. These blockers allow you to specify which websites or apps you want to limit access to during specific times or work sessions.

By using website blockers, you can prevent yourself from mindlessly visiting websites or social media platforms that tend to consume a lot of your time. It helps you maintain discipline and stay focused on your tasks without being tempted to check these distracting websites frequently.

In other words, website blockers act as a tool to enforce self-discipline, reducing the risk of getting sidetracked by online distractions and improving your ability to concentrate on the work at hand.

Step 3: Get Your Workspace Cleared Out and In Order

Make sure your desk is clear of anything that could divert your attention. If you have a list of things to do piling up on your desk, try moving them to a folder in a drawer. Don't be tempted to pick up your phone by having it sitting on your desk. Your workstation should be uncluttered and easy to work at. Don't use your desk as a storage space for games or books you might wish to read.

Step 4: Track Your Daily Activities

If you're at a loss to account for your time during the day, try keeping a detailed log of everything you do for a week. It's possible that your time-wasting and distractions will surprise you. Once you start keeping track of what you do, you may find that there are specific times and methods by which you become easily distracted.

Recognizing your own patterns is the first step toward altering how you act. Take a 15-minute stroll as an alternative to spending 30 minutes on social media.

If you notice that you get distracted during the day due to a lack of a perceived deadline, setting deadlines for yourself may assist. Setting a specific date and time by which you want to have completed a school or work-related activity can be a powerful motivator.

Step 5: Make Use of headphones

Noise levels at the workplace might be disruptive. Put on some headphones if outside noise is distracting you. To assist you in focusing, you may put on some tunes or use some noise-canceling headphones. Don't listen to music that makes you want to sing along or that distracts you from what you're doing. You should listen to music without vocals instead.

Step 6: Avoid Multi-Tasking

Multitasking can make some people feel more productive. But research shows that trying to do too much at once really makes you less efficient. It is often more efficient to devote one's full attention to a single task rather than switching back and forth between them. Don't multitask; focus on finishing one thing before moving on to the next. When you feel you're uncon-sciously jumping into something new, take a break.

Step 7: Practice the Two-Minute Rule

The "Two-Minute Rule" is a productivity technique designed to tackle small tasks quickly and efficiently. The idea behind this rule is simple: If a task can be completed in two minutes or less, you should do it immediately rather than putting it off for later. By adopting this approach, you can prevent small tasks from accumulating and becoming distractions that take up more mental space over time.

Here's how the Two-Minute Rule works:

- *Identify Small Tasks:* Pay attention to the tasks that come up throughout your day that can be completed quickly. These tasks typically require just a few minutes to accomplish.
- *Take Immediate Action:* When you encounter such a task, don't postpone it. Instead, complete it right away. This could be responding to a short email, filing a document, making a quick phone call, or tidying up your workspace.
- *Stay Focused:* While applying the Two-Minute Rule, make sure you stay focused on the task at hand. Resist the temptation to get sidetracked or move on to other unrelated tasks during these short bursts of productivity.

The benefits of the Two-Minute Rule are twofold:

1. *Quick Task Completion:* By promptly addressing small tasks, you prevent them from lingering on your to-do list. This helps you maintain a sense of accomplishment and keeps your workload manageable.
2. *Clearing Mental Clutter:* Eliminating these small tasks can help declutter your mind and free up mental space.

This, in turn, reduces the likelihood of these minor tasks becoming distractions that take your attention away from more critical or time-consuming activities.

NOTE: While the Two-Minute Rule is excellent for managing minor tasks efficiently, remember that it may not apply to more complex or time-intensive tasks. For larger tasks, consider breaking them down into smaller sub-tasks that can be completed within a few minutes each, and then apply the Two-Minute Rule to those sub-tasks.

Chapter 16
Step 9: Maintain Quality Nutrition And Sleep

Maintaining quality nutrition and adequate sleep can be beneficial for managing ADHD. While they may not directly treat ADHD symptoms, they can significantly impact overall well-being, attention, and focus, making it easier to manage the challenges associated with ADHD.

THE ROLE OF NUTRITION AND SLEEP IN ADHD MANAGEMENT

Both nutrition and sleep play essential roles in supporting overall cognitive function and emotional well-being. While they may not be standalone treatments for ADHD, they can complement other ADHD management strategies, such as behavioral therapy and medication.

1. NUTRITION

A. Balanced Diet

Focus on a balanced diet that includes a variety of nutrient-dense foods. Ensure you get enough fruits, vegetables, whole grains, lean proteins, and healthy fats. Proper nutrition supports brain function and provides essential nutrients for overall health.

B. Omega-3 Fatty Acids

Omega-3 fatty acids have been a topic of interest in research, and some studies have suggested potential benefits for individuals with ADHD, particularly in terms of cognitive function and behavior.

Here's a breakdown of Omega-3 fatty acids benefits:

- *Cognitive Function:* Omega-3 fatty acids, specifically EPA (eicosapentaenoic acid) and DHA (docosahexaenoic acid), are essential components of cell membranes in the brain. They play a crucial role in supporting brain structure and function. Some studies have indicated that a higher intake of omega-3 fatty acids may be associated with improved cognitive performance, including attention and memory.
- *Mood Regulation:* Omega-3 fatty acids have been linked to improved mood regulation and emotional well-being. People with ADHD may experience challenges with emotional regulation, and omega-3 supplementation might help support more stable moods.
- *Inflammation and Neuroprotection:* Omega-3 fatty acids possess anti-inflammatory properties and may

offer some neuroprotective effects. Reducing inflammation in the brain may positively impact cognitive function and potentially improve ADHD symptoms.

C. Protein-Rich Breakfast

Eating a protein-rich breakfast can help stabilize blood sugar levels and improve concentration throughout the day.

- *Stabilizing Blood Sugar Levels:* Protein-rich foods take longer to digest than carbohydrates. When you consume protein in the morning, it helps slow down the absorption of sugar into the bloodstream. This leads to a more gradual rise and fall in blood sugar levels, providing a steady source of energy throughout the morning. Stable blood sugar levels can prevent energy crashes and fluctuations that can affect focus and attention.
- *Enhanced Satiety:* Protein is known to increase feelings of fullness and satiety. By including protein in your breakfast, you may feel more satisfied and less likely to experience hunger or cravings later in the morning. This can prevent distractions caused by thoughts of food or the need to snack frequently.
- *Improved Cognitive Function:* Adequate protein intake supports the production of neurotransmitters in the brain. These chemicals are essential for transmitting signals between brain cells and are involved in various cognitive functions, including attention, memory, and concentration.
- *Balanced Nutrient Intake:* Protein-rich breakfast options often come with other essential nutrients, such

as vitamins, minerals, and healthy fats. A well-balanced breakfast can provide the necessary nutrients to support overall health and well-being.

- *Better Mood Regulation:* Protein intake can influence the production of serotonin, a neurotransmitter associated with mood regulation. A stable mood can positively impact focus and attention, making it easier to manage ADHD symptoms.

Here are some protein-rich breakfast options you might consider:

- *Eggs:* A classic and versatile source of protein. You can prepare them in various ways, such as scrambled, boiled, or as an omelet.
- *Greek Yogurt:* High in protein and calcium. Choose plain, unsweetened Greek yogurt and add fresh fruits or nuts for extra flavor and nutrients.
- *Nuts and Seeds:* Sprinkle nuts (e.g., almonds, walnuts) and seeds (e.g., chia seeds, flaxseeds) over your breakfast cereal or yogurt for an added protein boost.
- *Protein Smoothie:* Blend together a combination of fruits, vegetables, protein powder, and a liquid base (e.g., milk, almond milk) for a nutrient-dense breakfast option.
- *Nut Butter:* Spread natural nut butter (e.g., almond butter, peanut butter) on whole-grain toast for a protein-rich and satisfying breakfast.

REMEMBER: Everyone's nutritional needs are different, so it's essential to find breakfast options that work best for you and align with your preferences and dietary requirements.

D. Limit Sugar and Processed Foods

Limiting the consumption of sugary and highly processed foods can have significant benefits for overall health and well-being, including helping to manage ADHD symptoms, stabilizing energy levels, and preventing mood swings.

How does reducing sugar and processed foods positively impact energy levels, mood, and ADHD management? Let's find out:

- *Stable Energy Levels:* Sugary and processed foods, such as sugary snacks, pastries, and sugary beverages, cause a rapid spike in blood sugar levels. However, this spike is often followed by a quick drop in blood sugar, leading to energy crashes. These fluctuations can result in feelings of fatigue, irritability, and difficulty maintaining focus, which can be particularly challenging for individuals with ADHD.
- *Improved Mood Stability:* High sugar intake has been associated with mood swings and an increased risk of anxiety and depression. By reducing sugary and processed foods, you may experience more stable moods, which can positively impact emotional regulation and ADHD symptoms.
- *Focus and Attention:* Excessive sugar consumption has been linked to reduced cognitive performance and attention difficulties. Avoiding sugary and processed foods can help maintain better focus and concentration throughout the day.
- *Balanced Nutrition:* Processed foods are often low in essential nutrients and high in empty calories. By reducing their intake, you create more space for nutrient-dense whole foods, such as fruits, vegetables,

whole grains, and lean proteins, which support overall health, cognitive function, and emotional well-being.

- *Weight Management:* High consumption of sugary and processed foods can contribute to weight gain and obesity. Managing weight can positively impact overall health and may lead to improved ADHD symptoms.

To reduce sugar and processed foods in your diet, you can try the following tips:

- Opt for whole, unprocessed foods whenever possible. Choose fresh fruits, vegetables, whole grains, and lean proteins.
- Read food labels and avoid products with added sugars, high-fructose corn syrup, and artificial sweeteners.
- Limit the intake of sugary beverages like soda, fruit juices, and energy drinks. Opt for water, herbal tea, or infused water instead.
- Prepare meals at home using fresh ingredients, as this allows you to control the amount of sugar and additives in your food.
- When you have a sweet craving, try healthier alternatives like fresh fruit, a small piece of dark chocolate, or homemade snacks made with natural sweeteners like honey or maple syrup.

E. Stay Hydrated

Staying hydrated is essential for maintaining optimal cognitive function and overall health. Proper hydration supports various bodily functions, including brain function, and can positively impact attention, focus, and mood.

Importance of staying hydrated:

- *Brain Function:* The brain requires adequate hydration to function optimally. When you are dehydrated, brain cells may not communicate as effectively, leading to reduced cognitive performance, memory issues, and difficulty concentrating. Drinking enough water helps ensure that your brain stays alert and responsive.
- *Cognitive Performance:* Even mild dehydration can affect cognitive performance, including attention and reaction times. By staying hydrated, you can support your ability to focus, think clearly, and make better decisions.
- *Mood and Energy:* Dehydration can lead to feelings of fatigue and irritability, which can worsen ADHD symptoms. Staying hydrated can help maintain stable energy levels and a more positive mood, making it easier to manage the challenges of ADHD.
- *Physical Well-Being:* Proper hydration is essential for overall physical health. It helps regulate body temperature, aids digestion, supports cardiovascular function, and promotes better sleep—all of which can indirectly impact cognitive function and emotional well-being.
- *Avoiding Confusion with Thirst:* Thirst can be mistaken for hunger or restlessness, leading to unnecessary snacking or overeating. Drinking enough water throughout the day can help prevent these false signals and minimize potential distractions related to hunger or discomfort.

2. SLEEP

A. Consistent Sleep Schedule

A consistent sleep schedule means going to bed and waking up at the same time every day, including weekends. By following a regular sleep routine, you help your body's internal clock, also known as the circadian rhythm, to function optimally.

Importance of a consistent sleep schedule:

- **Regulating Sleep-wake Cycle:** Our bodies have a natural sleep-wake cycle, which is influenced by our daily habits and exposure to light and darkness. When you maintain a consistent sleep schedule, your body gets used to a predictable pattern, making it easier to fall asleep and wake up at the same time each day.
- **Improved Sleep Quality:** Having a regular sleep routine helps improve the overall quality of your sleep. When your body knows when to expect sleep, it prepares itself for rest, leading to more restorative and deep sleep.
- **Better Energy and Alertness:** Following a consistent sleep schedule can lead to increased daytime energy and alertness. This can be particularly helpful for individuals with ADHD, as proper sleep can positively impact attention and focus.
- **Balanced Hormones:** Adequate and regular sleep supports the regulation of various hormones in the body, including those that influence mood, appetite, and stress. A balanced hormonal system contributes to overall well-being.
- **Consistency Helps Reset Your Body Clock:** If you have experienced irregular sleep patterns due to travel, work

shifts, or other disruptions, getting back into a consistent sleep schedule can help reset your body's internal clock and improve sleep consistency.

B. Create a Relaxing Bedtime Routine

A pre-sleep routine is a set of calming activities you do before going to bed to help your body and mind relax. The purpose of this routine is to prepare yourself for sleep, signaling that it's time to wind down and get ready for rest.

By having a regular pre-sleep routine, you create a consistent signal to your body that bedtime is approaching. This helps your body's internal clock stay on track, making it easier to fall asleep at the same time each night.

Some relaxing pre-sleep activities include reading a book, taking a warm bath, or practicing deep breathing. These activities can help reduce stress and calm your mind, making it easier for you to fall asleep peacefully.

Having a pre-sleep routine also allows you to transition from the activities of the day to a more restful state gradually. This can be especially helpful for individuals with ADHD because it provides a structured way to wind down and detach from potential distractions.

C. Limit Screen Time Before Bed

The use of electronic devices before bedtime has been associated with poorer sleep quality and difficulties falling asleep. Poor sleep quality can worsen symptoms of ADHD, such as inattention and hyperactivity, and impact overall well-being.

Avoiding electronic devices such as smartphones, tablets, and computers at least an hour before bedtime is a helpful practice for improving sleep quality, especially for individuals with ADHD.

Electronic devices emit a type of light called "blue light." This blue light is similar to natural sunlight and can disrupt the body's natural sleep-wake cycle. When you use these devices close to bedtime, especially in a dark environment, the blue light signals to your brain that it's still daytime, suppressing the production of the sleep hormone melatonin.

Melatonin is a hormone that your body naturally produces in response to darkness. It helps regulate your sleep-wake cycle by making you feel sleepy and promoting deep sleep. Exposure to blue light from screens before bedtime can delay the release of melatonin, making it harder for you to fall asleep.

Optimize Sleep Environment

A comfortable sleep environment helps you feel at ease and relaxed when it's time to sleep. When you're comfortable, you're more likely to fall asleep faster and experience restful sleep throughout the night.

Tips for a Sleep-Conducive Environment:

- *Comfortable Bedding:* Invest in a comfortable mattress, pillows, and soft bedding that suits your preferences for support and comfort.
- *Blackout Curtains:* Install blackout curtains or shades in your bedroom to block out external light and create a dark sleep environment, particularly if you live in an area with bright outdoor lighting.
- *White Noise Machines:* If you're sensitive to noises, consider using a white noise machine to mask disruptive sounds. White noise can create a consistent and

175

soothing background sound that can drown out disturbances.

- *Earplugs:* If you live in a noisy environment or have trouble with external sounds, earplugs can help reduce noise disruptions during sleep.
- *Temperature Control:* Keep your bedroom at a comfortable temperature, usually slightly cooler than the rest of your home, to promote better sleep.
- *Declutter:* Clear your bedroom of unnecessary clutter to create a calming and organized sleep environment.

Limit Caffeine and Stimulants

Avoiding caffeine and other stimulants, especially in the afternoon and evening, is essential for managing ADHD and improving sleep quality. Stimulants like caffeine found in coffee, tea, energy drinks, and some medications can disrupt your body's natural sleep-wake cycle, making it harder to fall asleep and stay asleep.

When you consume stimulants close to bedtime, they can increase alertness, restlessness, and anxiety, preventing your mind and body from relaxing before sleep. This can lead to disrupted sleep patterns and poorer sleep quality, which can further impact ADHD symptoms and overall well-being.

Reducing stimulant intake is crucial for promoting better sleep and managing ADHD effectively. By avoiding caffeine and stimulants in the afternoon and evening, you can give your body enough time to process and eliminate these substances, allowing your natural sleep-wake cycle to function optimally.

Improved sleep quality can positively influence attention, focus, and mood, making it an essential component of ADHD management. To support better sleep, opt for caffeine-free beverages and herbal teas as alternatives, and create a relaxing pre-sleep routine to prepare your body and mind for rest. Establishing healthy sleep habits can lead to more restful nights and better daytime functioning for individuals with ADHD.

Chapter 17
Step 10: Medication

Stimulant medicine is typically the sole treatment required for people with ADHD. When used to treat ADHD, few interventions in all of medicine are as swiftly and radically beneficial as stimulant medication.

When it works, which it usually does, the child's improvement in behavior and functioning is nearly remarkable, and the child can accomplish better than he has ever done before. We've seen this happen time and time again, and we're sure that failing to treat the ADHD youngster effectively represents a huge missed opportunity. This may be the only treatment required for some children.

The stimulant drugs used to treat ADHD are classified into two types. These include amphetamines like Dexedrine, Adderall, and Vyvanse, as well as methylphenidates like Ritalin, Methylin, Metadate CD, Ritalin LA, Daytrana, Focalin XR, and Concerta. Amphetamine was first made available in the late 1930s.

Methylphenidate was discovered in 1955 and initially utilized in the early 1970s. As many as 80-90 percent of ADHD children benefit from one of these medications. These will be covered in detail later in the chapter.

Psychological and educational therapies, as addressed later in the chapter, may also be required for some ADHD youngsters. It is frequently difficult to predict how much better a youngster will be after taking medication. Some difficulties may subside after a kid has been treated with drugs, while others may persist. Psychological treatment for the family or educational intervention for the child with ADHD and learning impairments may also be beneficial at times.

CONCERNS ABOUT MEDICATION

The use of medication to treat children might be disturbing to parents at times. Parents are distressed for a variety of reasons, and it may be beneficial to discuss them. First, many parents struggle to accept that their child's behavior problems are physical rather than psychological in nature; this is generally due to their fear of medical problems. They believe a temper tantrum will pass quickly, but the chemically unbalanced brain may never recover. As a result, people prefer to believe that the problem is psychological. Behavior disorders having physical origins, like many other major physical problems, can occasionally be simply addressed. Psychological treatment, on the other hand, is not always as effective. Some psychological issues, for example, cannot be treated after years of costly and time-consuming psychiatric treatment.

Even if he later receives warm, caring parental care and counseling, a child who has been neglected or physically, sexually, or psychologically abused as a youngster may never function normally.

Another reason parents may oppose medication-assisted treatment is that it appears fake. It does not appear to be a good method to get to the bottom of the problem, according to many parents. That may be true if the cause of the problem is psychological, but in the case of ADHD, the cause is physical. Because certain of the brain's regulatory functions are not working as well as they should, pharmacological measures must be employed to increase their performance.

Medication can be thought of as a type of replacement therapy; that is, it appears to supply substances that are deficient or diminished, or it stimulates the body to produce more of the missing chemicals. At the moment, there is no pharmaceutical that may permanently correct the shortage. Medication is essential until the brain produces appropriate levels of the required chemicals as a result of its growth and development. ADHD children may outgrow these issues.

Another reason parents may reject medication is a fear that their child will become reliant on it. Despite their usefulness and safety, amphetamines and methylphenidate have a terrible reputation for causing adults to become euphoric and addicted to them. (Amphetamine is commonly referred to as "speed.") Stimulant medicines affect ADHD children and adults very differently than they do normal individuals. Instead of getting high or excited, these drugs normally calm down youngsters with ADHD, and they may occasionally (rarely) become depressed. These drugs are sometimes referred to be paradoxical because the stimulants have opposing effects on youngsters compared to non-ADHD adults.

Children do not develop hooked to these medications; there is no risk of this happening. Children may be pleased with the improvements to their life that medication brings, but they never like the medicine. It does not give them a high. They don't get a kick out of it. The fundamental question is whether the drug is helpful or detrimental.

As can be demonstrated, the majority of ADHD drugs are effective and pose little danger. If the ADHD child's difficulties linger into puberty, a few doctors will try to provide alternative medications, but these meds are rarely helpful. However, most physicians who have treated a large number of ADHD children continue to take stimulant drugs far into adolescence and adulthood because they are under the medical assumption that these people do not begin to respond to the drugs as quickly as normal non-ADHD adults.

Parents are also concerned about the continued usage of medicine to treat difficulties. This is, unfortunately, the nature of the sickness. Many ADHD children require medication to control their symptoms. The youngster with ADHD is in a comparable but less dangerous situation as the child with diabetes, epilepsy, or rheumatic fever. For the rest of their lives, children with these illnesses must take insulin, antiepileptic medications, or penicillin. The ADHD child may be more fortunate. Because many ADHD children outgrow their severe symptoms, an ADHD youngster may only need medication for a portion of his life.

We will attempt to help parents comprehend the physician's treatment aims by reviewing the key drugs used by most physicians in treating ADHD children, their effects, and their administration. We will not provide an entire list of medications, and this talk is not designed to empower parents to treat their children on their own. Parents who understand how a drug should operate, what side effects it can cause, and what (if any) potential risks come with its use are in a far better position to aid their doctors in treating their children. Keeping this in mind, let us now discuss some general elements of ADHD drug administration in children.

STIMULANT DRUGS

Stimulant medicine for ADHD may be the most effective psychiatric treatment. They are extremely beneficial and have the potential to change a child's life.

Effectiveness

Although both amphetamines and methylphenidate may be beneficial to children with ADHD, it is hard to predict how a child will react to a certain medicine. Although approximately the same number of children respond to each stimulant, some children respond favorably to one medicine but not to the other. If one doesn't work, try the other. However, after rigorous testing with both medications, it is expected that 80-90 percent of youngsters would respond well.

ADHD children generally:

- become calmer and less active;
- develop a longer span of attention;
- become less stubborn and easier to manage;
- are often more sensitive to the needs of others and much more responsive to discipline and the wishes of others;
- have longer fuses and fewer or no temper tantrums;
- experience fewer emotional ups and downs;
- show a decrease in impulsivity, waiting before they act, and may begin to plan ahead;
- demonstrate an improvement in school performance (listening, following instructions, completing tasks, getting better grades;

- improve their handwriting;
- increase frustration tolerance; and
- become less disorganized.

The ADHD child's response to stimulant treatment is typically markedly improved. Most alternative treatments, at most, return a patient to his previous level of functioning. Antidepressants, for example, may eliminate depression, mood stabilizers may control the ups and downs of bipolar disorder, and antipsychotics may stop strange thinking and hallucinations, but none allow a person to function better than he has ever functioned before, as stimulants used to treat ADHD frequently do.

Let me repeat: stimulants may allow an ADHD patient to operate better than he has in his entire life. When stimulants are beneficial, the transient psychological progress that happens varies from just slowing down or quitting. And that is a totally different effect than what the parent may have experienced with tranquilizers or stimulants if he does not have ADHD.

When used by healthy individuals, tranquilizers provide a soothing effect, whereas stimulants have an exhilarating effect. Neither medicine stabilizes mood, cools tempers, makes one more law-abiding, dampens impulsivity, or aids in planning as stimulants do in ADHD patients.

Because of the widespread effect of stimulant medicine on multiple psychological functions, child psychiatrists believe that the brain chemistry of persons with ADHD differs from that of others in some respects. The drug appears to compensate for this chemical difference at a fundamental level (as outlined in the previous chapter), influencing behavior in a variety of ways.

If the youngster responds to amphetamines and methylphenidate, the drugs usually take effect right away. In some cases, the effects stated may take up to a week or two to become apparent.

Dosage

Stimulants are drugs that act quickly, although they can exist in short-acting and long-acting forms. Short-acting methylphenidate-based medications release all of the medication at once and have a duration of 3 to 4 hours, whereas amphetamine-based drugs have a duration of 4 to 5 hours. Long-acting medications gradually release their drug over time and can last 8 to 12 hours. When only short-acting drugs were available, a youngster may have had to take 3-5 doses throughout the day. This could be made to function, but it usually resulted in a slew of social and logistical issues at school and at home. Fortunately, longer-acting versions have been created (and new ones are being developed all the time).

Modern treatment typically begins with the use of a long-acting drug first thing in the morning. It may last all day, which is wonderful. It may, however, wear off too quickly (for example, before schoolwork is completed in the afternoon), in which case it may need to be supplemented with a dose of a short-acting medicine. However, it may persist too long and disrupt sleep; thus, short-acting versions may be required instead. The goal is to find the best schedule or mix of long-acting and short-acting drugs to cover waking hours.

The doctor will also look for the lowest effective dose of medication because he or she does not want to administer more than is necessary. The youngster may not respond to the first dose tried (though this does happen) because it is too low. The dose is steadily increased until either the ADHD symptoms diminish or side effects emerge.

It may be essential to significantly increase the amount of medicine. This should not be cause for concern. Children vary tremendously, and some require significantly more medication than others. The amount of medication prescribed is not always proportional to the severity of the problem. For example, some ADHD children with severe symptoms may only require a little dosage of medication, whilst those with less severe symptoms may require a greater amount. In any case, if an effective regimen is established, minimal alterations are likely to be required.

The doctor's decision to increase or decrease the medication dose is heavily influenced by the parent's assessment of their child's functioning. The dosages that were originally used should be known to the parents. Medications are typically measured in milligrams (1 milligram equals 1/30,000 ounce). An ADHD child's amphetamine requirements typically range from 10 to 30 mg per day. Because methylphenidate is half as strong as amphetamines, the daily dose can range from 20 to 60 mg. There are occasional exceptions in either way.

Parents must understand that the effects of stimulant medicines are very temporary. There is no carryover from one day to the next for amphetamines and methylphenidate. When the drug is working, the parents will notice that if it is stopped for a day, the child's temperamental issues will reappear. As a result, the child's ADHD may be present in the morning until his medicine is administered. If he is sluggish in getting dressed, having break-fast, and getting to school, it may be beneficial or required to give him the prescription as soon as he awakens.

Similarly, because the medications are typically used in quanti-ties that allow the effects to wear off in the late afternoon or early evening, parents may anticipate increased trouble with the child at that time. If the parent's primary interaction with the child is just after the child returns home from school, the parent may believe that the medicine is ineffective. To check on this, the parent should closely observe the child's behavior during the weekend, especially in the mornings and early afternoons, when the medicine is most active.

This will also allow the parent to carefully examine how long each dose lasts, which will aid the doctor in determining the appropriate dose spacing. If the child has homework to do after school, or if parents plan to take the child out in the evening or to a large family event, a modest additional dose later in the afternoon is generally useful.

After starting with the smallest dose of medication that has been found to be effective with ADHD children of the child's age, the physician will usually follow the principle of gradually increasing the medication until either the child's behavioral problems improve to the greatest extent possible or the side effects of the increased dosages cause a problem in themselves. The physician will want to know what is going on at home and school to determine how much help the child is receiving. Because he or she sees the child in situations where he or she is likely to have the most difficulties, the schoolteacher is in a good position to identify the effects of the medicine. Furthermore, the teacher can compare his conduct to that of a large number of other children his age and intellectual level. It is a good idea for the parent to contact the instructor anytime the medication is altered or changed.

The parent should inform the teacher that the child is undergoing treatment and request a report on any changes in the child's classroom behavior that the teacher may detect. In practice, it is best not to make a big deal out of this type of information. Most individuals who expect to see changes see them even if they are not present, so the parent should just request information rather than suggesting that the teacher expects to see the child improve. Another reason for avoiding implying that the child would improve is that many teachers, in order to spare parents' feelings, will fail to mention any difficulties they may be having at school.

If the child improves slightly and is no longer a serious issue, the teacher may advise the parent that things are going "pretty well." The parent wants to know whether there are any issues, what kind they are, and how serious they are. There are various standardized questionnaires available for teachers, and they are quite useful in alerting parents and doctors about the child's progress.

The timing of the medication will be determined by the type of problems that the ADHD child is experiencing. Parents will undoubtedly play an important role in this process. For example, symptoms may lessen as the child grows older. As previously said, parents should keep in mind that while hyperactivity and restlessness may diminish, other issues, such as poor concentration and underachievement, may persist. As a result, parents should request specific information from the teacher.

It is insufficient to know that the child is not restless. How he interacts with his classmates, how he concentrates on his tasks, how much work he can complete, and how well he does it must all be constantly scrutinized. Even a child with ADHD and learning difficulty may experience an improvement in his work, while stimulants have no direct influence on such learning issues. This progress happens as a result of increased focus, attention, and productivity, which frequently leaves the youngster more accessible to remedial education. (As an added bonus, his penmanship may improve.)

The goal of administering medication is more than simply controlling the child's behavior and allowing him to acclimate to a setting he dislikes and in which he performs poorly: school.

Effective medication frequently grants the youngster self-control. In some ways, he will have more freedom, not less, and will have fewer symptoms such as moodiness and aggression. He will be loved more by instructors, parents, siblings, and peers if he is less pushy, more obedient (without becoming a robot!), cooler-tempered, and a better student. He'll be happier with himself and his life. More than only his academic performance improves. His situation improves.

One last point. As previously stated, unlike people without ADHD, children normally do not acquire resistance to the effects of these drugs, but some tolerance may develop during the first few weeks of treatment. In such cases, the pharmaceutical dosage that offered relief from symptoms for a month or so gradually fails to control those symptoms. The doctor will normally increase the medication if there is no additional development of tolerance. If a youngster is on medication for several years, he may occasionally require an increased dose of medication as he grows older and larger.

Because adults can abuse amphetamines and methylphenidate, the government strictly regulates their prescribing. They cannot be called into the pharmacy; instead, they must get a written prescription for one month only, though in some jurisdictions, the physician may write and future date up to two extra prescriptions.

Side Effects

Many drugs have negative side effects. A side effect is an unintended consequence of taking medication. Aspirin, for example, might cause stomach lining irritation and minor abdominal pain in some people. Antihistamines used to treat hay fever might produce tiredness. Stimulant drugs are unusually safe medications when administered to children, yet, they can occasionally cause negative effects. These will be described further below.

Stimulant medicines reduce hunger and interfere with sleep in both children and adults. The child's decreased appetite usually, but not always, lasts as long as the drug is active and may be followed by some weight loss. Although this weight loss may cause alarm among parents, it is seldom medically significant. (After the medication wears off, children's appetites usually return in the evening.

As a result, they should be permitted to eat as much as they want after dinner. Of course, appetite will be normal during breakfast before the drug takes effect.) The child may complain of a stomachache and decreased appetite when initially starting on stimulants, but these adverse effects normally go away quickly. The drug's proclivity to keep some youngsters awake may usually be managed by carefully scheduling its delivery. Medication only keeps youngsters awake while it is still in their bloodstream (8-12 hours for most long-acting versions). This is why these medications should not be administered late in the day. Sleeplessness will not be an issue if the drug is properly regulated.

However, as the drug wears off, behavioral issues may emerge later in the day. Insomnia may usually be avoided by allowing the final dose to wear off (in 3- 4 hours) before the child goes to bed. If insomnia persists and the kid struggles with behavioral control at bedtime, the doctor may suggest that the last dose be administered earlier in the day.

If insomnia is a significant problem, the doctor may sometimes recommend taking other medications before going to bed. At bedtime, Catapres (clonidine) and Intuniv (guanfacine) can be used. These medications chemically prevent the stimulating effects of stimulants, allowing the youngster to sleep. Both medicines may pose safety risks, and their usage should be reviewed with a physician.

A new study found that children and adolescents with ADHD who had structural heart abnormalities or other significant heart diseases, such as heart rhythm or muscle disorders, have an increased chance of having a cardiac event. Cardiac incidents are more common in people with similar cardiac issues, such as severe coronary artery disease. Although this risk was first thought to be associated with stimulant usage, this no longer appears to be the case.

Stimulants have been linked to the development of tic disorders in children; however, this does not appear to be the case. Children who already have modest tics may have them worsen with stimulants, but they usually go away once the medicine is stopped.

It may not be easy to know when to stop raising the stimulant dose. When the dose is too high, the youngster may experience melancholy or a decrease in appetite, and he may become increasingly irritable and fussy. These are indications that the dose should be reduced.

STIMULANT MEDICATIONS AND GROWTH

A study published several years ago found that stimulant drugs slowed the pace of growth in ADHD youngsters, both in height and weight. Several further research on the same topic have been published since that report. It appears that the growth rate has slowed for one to two years. Following that, the growth rate appears to be approaching normal, and there appears to be no reduction in height among ADHD teenagers.

The situation is difficult since ADHD children may have different growth patterns than typical children, and standard growth tables may not apply to ADHD children. Doctors who have used stimulants to treat ADHD children from childhood to puberty have found no long-term impact of stimulant treatment on height. When medicine is interrupted during summer holidays, growth normally resumes, but medication should be restored if there is severe deterioration in behavior.

There is little doubt that stimulant treatment causes many ADHD children to lose weight. Although this can be disappointing for parents, there is no evidence that it is hazardous, and weight normally returns to normal after the medicine is discontinued. We should highlight that the reported impacts are minor and that most physicians treating ADHD children believe that the psychological advantages outweigh any potential effects on growth rate. On a practical level, the physician must monitor the child's height, weight, and adjustment changes and base the usage of stimulant medication on its influence on growth and the child's psychological well-being.

NON-STIMULANT DRUGS

There are some other non-stimulant medicines that are infrequently used to treat ADHD and may be beneficial for a few patients, but they are generally far less successful than stimulants.

Strattera (atomoxetine) is the FDA's first non-stimulant drug approved for the treatment of ADHD. It is usually taken once a day, in the morning. It has a number of annoying side effects, including drowsiness, exhaustion, decreased appetite, headache, and gastrointestinal distress, which can be extremely severe in some people.

Although it is significantly less effective than stimulants, it may be the first medicine to attempt in patients who do not respond to stimulants. Catapres (clonidine) is a medicine used to treat hypertension (high blood pressure) that has also been used to treat aggressive ADHD youngsters and as a nightly sedative in children who are getting stimulants and experiencing insomnia as a result of the stimulants. It is only moderately effective, and it takes about two weeks for its therapeutic impact to kick in. It has various side effects, including sleepiness and fatigue, dizziness, constipation, and reduced blood pressure, and it must be discontinued gradually to avoid a severe blood pressure increase.

Intuniv (guanfacine) is also licensed to treat ADHD. In terms of effectiveness and adverse effects, it is fairly comparable to clonidine; however, it may be better tolerated. Its efficacy is likewise restricted.

AIDS TO ADMINISTERING MEDICINE

Many parents are unaware that there are psychological components to administering and taking medicine. Most drugs are either for medical conditions or for obvious psychological ones; thus, this is typically disregarded. People use aspirin for headaches, laxatives for constipation, and tranquilizers for anxiety. The hows and whys are self-evident. However, certain psychological factors are key in the delivery of ADHD medication to youngsters. These rules must be followed correctly if treatment is to be as effective as possible.

First, the child must comprehend why he is being given medication. Second, he must be informed that taking medication does not imply that his problems are catastrophic, such as being brain-damaged, stupid, bad, or insane.

Third, it is beneficial to help him realize and accept faults in his own conduct that he does not like so that he does not feel as if the medicine is being provided to him solely to make other people tolerate him better. Assume a child does not understand why he is being given medication. In such instances, if he does not believe he has difficulties and that the drug is assisting him in dealing with them, he is more likely to resist taking it, forget to take it, or cease it as he ages but may still require it.

Typically, an ADHD youngster will notice and address aspects of his experience and conduct that he dislikes or that bring him into difficulty. These may include being unable to pay attention, having a strong temper, being "nervous" (restless), or being chastised by teachers or parents for forgetting things, not finishing work, or constantly leaving the classroom seat. He can be assured that the medication will assist him in completing his coursework, paying attention, maintaining his temper, being less nervous, remembering things better, and calming down. A significant task has been completed if he can acknowledge that the drug is helping him. He will have the impression that something is being done for him rather than against him.

It is equally critical when giving medicine to children that they do not believe they are exempt from responsibility for their own behavior because they must take medicine. ADHD, like any other disorder, does not imply a lack of free choice. It may restrict or modify a person's behavioral options, but it does not absolve them of all responsibility.

Children can and should believe that they share responsibility for their actions. They should not blame all of their behavior on forces outside their control. They should not be permitted to engage in the type of "game" that Eric Berne refers to as "wooden leg" in his book Games People Play. In this psychological game, the participant says something along the lines of "What can you expect of me?" I couldn't do anything else. "I have a wooden leg." Children should be discouraged from adopting the same approach toward their ADHD.

They should not be allowed to say things like, "I am a psychological cripple." I suffer from ADHD. "I have no control over my actions." As a result, parents (as well as teachers, brothers and sisters) should not explain the ADHD child's conduct solely on whether or not he has taken his medication.

"You're acting up," his parents should not say. "When did you get your medication?" Putting things this way gives the youngster the impression that he has little control over himself, and it may lead him to assume that his "badness" is explained by the absence of medicine and his "goodness" is explained by its presence. If that's the case, he can't take credit for self-control, and when he doesn't behave appropriately, he can frequently blame it on not taking his prescription.

Assume that while speaking with the ADHD youngster, his parents, teachers, or siblings frequently correlate his conduct with his medication regimen. In that case, he'll quickly learn how to play "medicine wooden leg": "What can you expect of me? "I have ADHD, and my medication is no longer effective."

The significance of explaining to children their responsibility for their behavior will be highlighted in the section of this chapter titled "Psychological Management."

THE BROADER APPROACH TO THE ADHD CHILD

The treatment of the ADHD youngster is frequently uncomplicated. Because medication is so important, treatment always necessitates the services of a physician. Nonmedical specialists, such as psychologists and social workers, can be helpful, but they cannot take sole responsibility for therapy.

They cannot provide the best and, in some cases, the only treatment because they are not educated to use and cannot prescribe pharmaceuticals. The ADHD child may cause family problems, which may drive the family to seek help, and these problems may resolve themselves once treatment begins. It is likely that the parents of an ADHD child are experiencing marital troubles; if only the parents are helped, the youngster will probably be more comfortable in some aspects, but his underlying problems will remain unaffected.

However, because ADHD is inherited, the parent may have ADHD, and the parent's own symptoms (such as being irritable, disorganized, or impulsive) sometimes interfere with the parent's ability to nurture an ADHD child. Treatment of ADHD—or any psychiatric disorder—in the parent will almost certainly be of tremendous aid in enabling the parent to care for the child adequately.

The MTA research (Multimodal therapy research of Children with ADHD), the most thorough scientific investigation of ADHD therapy yet conducted, proved the importance of medication as the first-line treatment.

It looked at 579 children with ADHD mixed type who were separated into equal groups and treated for 14 months with either medication management, rigorous behavioral treatment, or both, or treatment from community providers.

To ensure a fair trial of the behavioral treatment, the children who received it received a truly impressive combination of interventions: 35 group and individual family sessions; an 8-week, five days a week, nine hours a day summer program for the child with behavioral management and social skills training among other methods, and a classroom experience that taught academic skills and good classroom behavior; and a school-based program with 10- 16 sessions of teacher consultation.

This was more intensive care than the child would have gotten in the community. The children treated with medication, on the other hand, received only medication, usually stimulants, for 14 months, whilst the third group of children received both intense treatment and medication. At the end of the trial, children treated with medication alone and those treated with medication and therapy both exhibited significant and equal improvement in their core ADHD symptoms of inattention, impulsivity, and hyperactivity, but children treated with therapy alone showed only small improvement. Medication is recognized as an important treatment for ADHD children based on this type of data.

Finally, the same concepts apply to educational treatment. The educational psychologist at school will see the child if he or she has educational or behavioral issues or both. The counselor may believe that behavioral difficulties cause academic problems or that academic problems cause behavioral problems. In either situation, the counselor is probably somewhat correct.

The catch is that ADHD can create both types of issues or, more crucially, ADHD can be exacerbated by the learning deficits that frequently accompany it. Both of these illnesses must be identified and treated as soon as they appear. Only by addressing these underlying issues can the youngster receive the greatest treatment for his academic difficulties.

PSYCHOLOGICAL MANAGEMENT

Medication can help the majority of ADHD children. Understanding and consistent parenting and care can help all of them. ADHD children have specific challenges, but they might also have "unspecial" problems like any other child. Difficulties, misunderstandings, and tension between parent and kid are problematic for any child, but they may be especially problematic for the ADHD child.

As we have attempted to demonstrate, he does have psychological issues, but they are driven by physical factors.

How should a parent approach the situation? If an issue is psychological, it appears that the youngster is responsible for his actions. He should be commended if he is good and punished if he is terrible. Similarly, if the issue is physical, the youngster is not liable for his actions. If such is the case, he should not be rewarded or punished for being good. Neither of these assertions is correct. Temperament can have an impact on conduct, but it is not the only component that influences behavior. A child's temperament can make it easier or harder for him to regulate himself. It may make learning to respond to discipline simpler for him. However, how the parents feel about their child and how they treat him might have a significant impact.

Psychiatrists and psychologists have discovered in recent years that individuals with severe psychological issues that are physiologically caused can benefit significantly from certain psychological treatments. These methods are founded on three principles:

1. making the patients responsible for their behavior;
2. rewarding them for good behavior; and
3. punishing them (in a special way) for bad behavior.

The ADHD child performs better when he is held accountable for his actions. He should not be able to state, directly or indirectly, "I'm ADHD—I'm a mental cripple—I'm not responsible for what I do." He should be addressed as responsible and, if required, informed of something to the effect of: "You do have problems that make it difficult for you to control yourself at times." But the same is true for everyone. Everyone accomplishes some things more readily than others and struggles with others. I expect you to learn to (count to 10, control your temper, and not torment your sister)." Of course, like with all of our suggestions, parents should modify the wording to fit themselves and their children.

The youngster should not be considered irresponsible or blame-worthy but rather as someone who has a higher proclivity than the average to experience various types of issues.

Parents should understand that no approach to childrearing will erase the central ADHD symptoms in the majority of ADHD youngsters. Regardless of parental discipline, the youngster will be more attention-seeking and forgetful and will appear absent-minded and stubborn. Most of the time, he is not doing these things intentionally to bother you. He would do things regardless of how he was raised. Parents should distinguish between symptoms that can be helped by both parental care and medicine and those that can only be helped by medicine. It will discourage parents from attempting to change items that cannot be changed (or can only be changed very little) in this manner.

Short attention span, distractibility, moodiness, lack of stick-to-itiveness, school underachievement, and immaturity are typical psychologically irreversible signs. Bedwetting, soiling, and anti-social activities such as theft are examples. Although psychological treatments may not always totally eliminate these issues in children, they can help to change them.

In essence, parents must keep three things in mind. One, the child struggles with doing and not doing specific things. Two, if he is treated as a responsible person who can gradually learn to manage himself and his conduct, he will learn best how to compensate for his problems. Three, the extent to which specific childrearing practices can assist him differs. Teaching him to control his temper or accept responsibility for his tasks is far easier than teaching him to have a longer attention span or be less distractible. Medicine and discipline will both help with the first type of difficulty (e.g., temper and chores). For the most part, only drugs can help with the second type of problem (e.g., short attention span).

Chapter 18
Helpful General Principles And Techniques

Numerous books have been written on the general topic of how parents should treat their children and relate to them in order to create the best possible psychological environment. They contain a wealth of good information for parents of all types of children, and no attempt is made here to review every strategy that psychologists have found useful. However, we will briefly explore some general ideas and approaches that are beneficial to both ADHD children and children who do not have any difficulties.

When combined with the prior description of basic methods, they paint a clear picture of psychological approaches that can be very beneficial in the management of the ADHD child.

How to Criticize

Children, like everyone else, dislike criticism. Everyone is more tolerant of criticism when it is particular rather than generic. For example, if a spouse comes home from work and finds supper not ready, he or she could say one of two things: "You are a disorganized person who never gets anything done," or "I'm always starving after work, and I'd really appreciate it if you could have dinner ready when I get home." The at-home spouse may not agree with any of the two comments, but the second is much easier to swallow because it is more detailed and somewhat more understanding. Similarly, an employer confronted with the difficulty of chastising an employee who is late finishing a piece of work could choose one of the following statements: "Jones, you are a lousy worker" or "Jones, I'd appreciate it in the future if you'd be faster getting me these reports." Again, the employee may be offended by any criticism, but the second version, in particular, is simpler to stomach.

The same logic applies to child criticism. When an ADHD child, for example, hits his baby sister for taking up his favorite toy, reducing her to a screaming mass, the parent is likely to erupt and shout things like, "Why must you be such a bad child?" "You're a terrible child who is always causing trouble!" "Can't you ever do anything right?" This is an understandable reaction.

Nonetheless, such an outburst is counterproductive. Parents are significantly better positioned to criticize explicitly if they have considered the problem areas where improvement is desired. For example, "I do not like it when you eat with your hands—that is for small babies, not big children"; "Mommy gets upset when she asks you to clean up your room, and you do not." Nobody likes looking at cluttered spaces. Please return and clean it." The father shows displeasure in the cases presented, but only for specific acts. It is entirely normal and reasonable for a parent to address feelings that a child is aware of.

The child can tell that his or her parent is upset. It is pointless to deny what the youngster knows. However, the parents must not allow their rage to manifest itself by criticizing the child as a whole. Parents must never label their children as useless or bad. When criticism is required, parents should be as explicit as possible in their disapproval of the unacceptable behavior.

How to Praise

Similarly, praise should be targeted. When the youngster is acting well, he or she should be lavished with affection. If the youngster is eating well, tell him or her, "You are eating in a very grown-up manner, and that pleases me." If his younger sister is taunting him and he has resisted the impulse to slug her, tell him, "I am very pleased that you can hold your temper even when Susie is making a pest of herself."

It's not useful to tell your child, "You're a wonderful child," or your spouse, "Jimmy has been just marvelous today." Such comments, in addition to being unhelpful in teaching the child self-control, are likely to come across as false to him.

Such broad praise strikes all of us as phony. We're all aware that we have flaws and that anyone who calls us "wonderful" is either trying to flatter us or call us foolish. The same reaction occurs in children. Consider a television chat program where an actor is presented as having a "wonderful personality." Most of us are turned off by that. We know it for what it is: nonsense. As a result, when you praise children, reward them for specific things they know are excellent. Please do not enlarge. Children perceive and value honesty.

Recognizing the Child's Feelings

The main premise here is that children, like adults, require under-standing, particularly from someone close to them. Children have emotions. Recognizing such feelings and informing the youngster that you are aware of them can frequently make them feel better. However, it is critical to understand that a parent can perceive and explain a child's feelings without scolding or praising him. Assume the child is returning from his room, where he was sent due to a lack of control. In that scenario, the parent can assist by saying, "You must have felt that it is very difficult for a seven-year-old to always remember his table manners, and you must have been angry at Mommy for making you leave the table."

The parent might make the youngster feel more at ease by noticing and neutrally acknowledging feelings.

Assisting the Child in Differentiating Between Feelings and Actions

The main point here is that feelings may and should be expressed, even when they are negative. Feelings and deeds are not the same thing, according to the same premise. Children, like adults, frequently have feelings that "they should not" have; they can be envious, jealous, furious, or resentful. These are sentiments that all children experience. Everyone has them in certain situations. Children frequently feel guilty for having such feelings. They've learned not to be envious, jealous, furious, or resentful. As previously indicated, it is quite useful if the parents acknowledge to themselves that the child has such feelings (when he does) and let the youngster know that they (the parents) are aware. Parents must assist their children in distinguishing between acceptable feelings and unacceptable acts. Actions or behavior may be changed and sculpted; sentiments, on the other hand, cannot and should not be treated as if they can. If the youngster sees that his parents recognize and tolerate his feelings, he may feel less anxious about having them.

His relief alone may frequently be enough to dissuade the child from acting on his negative emotions. If the youngster understands that terrible ideas do not imply that he is bad and worthless in his parent's eyes, he will feel less guilty. Because he has previously acted in ways that were deemed inappropriate, he is likely to see having equivalent ideas as equally heinous. Parents should frequently express to their child, both directly and indirectly, that any negative thoughts he may have are not that horrible if he does not act on them. He will occasionally be quite furious at his newborn sister; he should vent this anger, and his parents should assist him in doing so. He should not strike his younger sister. Parents should assist their children in understanding the distinction between thinking and doing.

The Technique of Labeling

Labeling is a very significant method for assisting the ADHD youngster in recognizing and dealing with his behavioral issues. Before the youngster can even attempt to control his conduct, he must first recognize when he is doing something that is bothersome to others and harmful to himself.

The problem is that many of these items are quite intricate. A parent can easily inform a child, "When you lie down on the floor, scream, or pound your heels, that is a tantrum," and "Mommy will not talk to you until the tantrum is over, and if you cannot make it stop quickly, you will have to go to your room until it is over." A three-year-old can comprehend the concept of a tantrum. However, some of the ADHD child's problematic behaviors are more complex. For example, he may design complex tactics for annoying his brother and sister and have a variety of them. His father and mother are unable to compile a comprehensive list of bothersome behaviors.

An entrepreneurial, intelligent ADHD youngster might find numerous ways to irritate people. Parents should establish a code word to help their child identify and recognize such behaviors. We utilize the code phrases "bugging" and "teasing."

When the ADHD child annoys his brother or sister in this manner, the child is reprimanded, "You are teasing." After a few dozen repeats — and parents will have many, many opportunities — the youngster learns that teasing refers to a wide range of behaviors. It is no more difficult for the child to understand this than it is to understand that Great Danes, Dachshunds, and Chihuahuas are all dogs.

Once the child understands what teasing is, the parents can broaden the procedure's utility by responding with fresh incidents differently. When Billy pretends to have misplaced his sister's toy, his parents can ask him, "Billy, what are you doing?" The plan is now for him to label his conduct, which is a step toward accepting more responsibility for it.

Labeling is an effective strategy for a variety of common difficulties, such as difficulty paying attention or being overly excited. Parents should actively seek out and create labels for their ADHD child's specific difficulties that could benefit from this technique. With this type of repetitive labeling, the ADHD child's parents can generally assist him in identifying what he is doing. This is not going to be simple. Even grownups who do not have ADHD do not readily notice the various ways they can be neurotic or unpleasant. It is not surprising that a ten-year-old will have difficulties understanding what is wrong with his actions.

The scientific study of the value of training youngsters to understand their problematic behavior is in its early stages. Interestingly, Russian child psychologists have been studying how language might help a youngster manage himself for some time. They believe that self-labeling is the first step toward self-management and that the sooner a child learns to label his actions, the sooner he can learn to regulate himself. Although clear data is not yet available, our clinical experience has convinced us that labeling as an additional parental method is effective.

Conclusion

It has been an inspiring journey. My guess is that you have been fully equipped with the necessary strategies and steps to help you manage your ADHD effectively.

This book has been an eye-opener as it explored the multifaceted world of Attention Deficit Hyperactivity Disorder (ADHD) and provided a comprehensive understanding of this condition.

In this book, we have looked into various aspects of ADHD, such as the fundamentals of ADHD, gaining insights into its symptoms, challenges, and prevalence in both children and adults. Understanding the intricacies of ADHD sets the stage for the transformative journey ahead.

In addition, we looked at the different types of ADHD, offering a nuanced perspective on its subtypes and their unique characteristics. By recognizing the distinctions between inattentive, hyperactive-impulsive, and combined presentations, we gain a deeper understanding of how ADHD manifests uniquely in each individual.

Conclusion

Also, this book takes an in-depth look at the possible causes of ADHD, considering genetic, environmental, and neurobiological factors. Understanding the origins of ADHD equips readers with a more comprehensive perspective, leading to personalized approaches for managing symptoms.

In all, the book provides us with a detailed 10-step guide to managing ADHD, such as establishing rules, rewards/punishments, structured routines, time management strategies, organization skills, exercise and physical activity, mindfulness and meditation, limiting distractions, maintaining quality nutrition and sleep, and medication.

With the general principles and techniques this book provides at the end, we are better guided and equipped with the necessary tips to better manage ADHD, whether as a kid or an adult.

Dear Reader,

Congratulations on finishing this book, I know you will now be well equipped for managing your Adhd. As I write these final words, I am filled with gratitude for the time we've spent together.

However, I have a humble request before we part ways, . Your personal experience with this book is invaluable, and I would be happy if you could take a moment to share it on Amazon. This is the number one thing you can do to help out me or any other independent author. Your review has the power to touch the lives of those who are yet to embark on this adventure.

To leave feedback on Amazon, simply navigate to the book's page and click on the "Write a Customer Review" button.

Conclusion

Now it's time to implement the 10 step system!

Thank you,

Gabrielle Townsend

Bibliography

Amanda, A. (2022). Adult ADHD: A Guide to Understanding And Managing ADHD in Adults. Rivercat Books LLC.

Andrew, B. (2019). Adult ADHD: A Comprehensive Guide to Attention Deficit Hyperactivity Disorder in Adults. Ingram Publishing.

Ashley, B. (2013). Adult ADHD Treatment: The Pros and Cons: How to Treat ADHD Effectively. Gold Crown.

Ben, H. (2020). Adult ADHD: The Complete Guide to Living With, Understanding, Improving, and Managing ADHD or ADD as an Adult. Ingram Publishing.

Charles, P. (2012). New ADHD Medication Rules: Brain Science & Common Sense. Koehler Studios, Inc.

Daniel, M. (2021). ADHD: The Complete Guide to Positive Parenting to Empower Your Kid (Non-medication Treatments and Skills for Children). Gary W. Turner.

Douglas, M. (2021). ADHD: Everything You Need to Know About Brain Stimulation (Raising Healthy and Emotionally Intelligent Kids Without Fear). Ademaro Rascon.

Foster, O. (2020). Attention-Deficit/Hyperactivity Disorder, Second Edition. Chelsea House.

Heather, F. (2020). ADHD: Symptoms and Solutions for Men And Women with Attention Deficit Hyperactivity Disorder. Efalon Acies.

James, P. (2020). Understanding ADHD: What causes ADHD And how to deal with it. Ingram Publishing.

Jeannine, H. (2018). Understanding And Treating ADHD. Jeannine.

John, R. (2021). Attention Deficit/Hyperactivity Disorder, Screen Time, Physical Activity, And Diet Quality: An Essay. Vincenzo Nappi.

Julia, K. (2019). The Adult ADHD & ADD Solution - Discover How to Restore Attention and Reduce Hyperactivity in Just 14 Days. Native Publisher.

Kay, J. (2014). Attention Deficit Hyperactivity Disorder (Adhd): You May Have It. Don't Let It Stop You. Xlibris AU.

Madeline, H. (2021). ADHD: Inside the Distracted Mind - The Brain Trap of the DMN & TPN. Madeline Holden.

Margaret, H. (2022). ADHD 2.0 & Social Anxiety for Adults: The 7-day Revolution. Margaret Hampton.

Bibliography

Nicoladie, T. (2013). ADHD/ADD: Attention Deficit Hyperactivity Disorders: A Tutorial Study Guide. Nicoladie Tam, Ph.D.

Quincy, F. (2015). ADHD: Attention Deficit Hyperactivity Disorder: The 21st century illness? MB Cooltura.

Scott, G. (2015). ADHD Adult: How to Recognize & Cope with Adult ADHD In 30 Easy Steps. Scott Green.

Stephen, C. (2021). ADHD: A Complete Guide for Adults to Understand ADHD (Impulse Control and Disorganization Through a Mind Process for a New Life). Stephen Allen.

Printed in Great Britain
by Amazon